BHAKTI YOGA & RAJA YOGA

Swami Vivekananda

Pharos Books

ISBN: 978-93-6700-717-4

©Publishers
Publisher: Pharos Books (P) Ltd.
Plot No.-63, 1st Floor, Main Mother Dairy Road
Pandav Nagar, East Delhi-110092
Phone: +14049995474, 011-40395855
WhatsApp: +91 9319228272
E-mail: sales@pharosbooks.in
Website: www.pharosbooks.in

Edition: 2025

Printed By: Sushma Book Binding House, Okhla
Industrial Area, Phase II, New Delhi-110020

Bhakti-Yoga and Raja-Yoga
By : Swami Vivekananda

Swami Vivekananda

Swami Vivekananda (1863-1902), born as Narendranath Datta in Kolkata, India, is revered as one of India's most influential spiritual leaders and a key figure in the introduction of Indian philosophies of Vedanta and Yoga to the Western world. A disciple of the saint Ramakrishna Paramahamsa, Swami Vivekananda played a crucial role in reviving Hinduism, advocating for social reforms, and fostering interfaith harmony. His legacy is far-reaching, touching upon religion, spirituality, education, and nationalism, and his thoughts continue to inspire people across the globe.

Early Life and Education

Born on January 12, 1863, into a well-educated and aristocratic Bengali family, Narendranath showed signs of intellectual brilliance and deep spirituality from an early age. His father, Vishwanath Datta, was a successful attorney with a progressive outlook, while his mother, Bhuvaneshwari Devi, was deeply religious and instilled in him strong moral values and devotion to the divine. Vivekananda's inquisitive nature led him to study a wide range of subjects, from Western philosophy and history to Sanskrit scriptures. He was particularly influenced by the works of the English poet William Wordsworth and the writings of Ralph Waldo Emerson, John Stuart Mill, and Herbert Spencer.

However, his search for spiritual truth went beyond academic learning. Vivekananda was deeply troubled by the social inequalities, poverty, and religious dogmatism in India. His spiritual quest led him to Ramakrishna, a mystic and saint from Dakshineswar, whose teachings would change the course of his life.

Association with Ramakrishna

Vivekananda's meeting with Ramakrishna in 1881 marked the beginning of a transformative spiritual journey. Ramakrishna taught him that all religions lead to the same ultimate truth and that service to humanity was the greatest form of worship. Under his guidance, Vivekananda learned about Advaita Vedanta, which emphasizes the oneness of the soul (Atman) and the Divine (Brahman). After Ramakrishna's death in 1886, Vivekananda, along with his fellow disciples, established the Ramakrishna Order, dedicated to serving humanity and spreading the spiritual wisdom of their master.

Spiritual Wanderer and the Chicago Parliament of Religions

After renouncing worldly life, Vivekananda travelled across India as a wandering monk between 1888 and 1893.

His travels exposed him to the plight of the poor and the deep spiritual hunger of the Indian masses. This experience shaped his vision of social service and spiritual upliftment, reinforcing his belief that the alleviation of poverty and ignorance was essential for India's resurgence.

In 1893, Vivekananda travelled to the United States, where he delivered a historic speech at the Parliament of the World's Religions in Chicago. His opening words, "Sisters and Brothers of America," and his message of universal brotherhood and tolerance for all religions received a standing ovation and established him as an eloquent spokesperson for India's spiritual heritage. He introduced the Western world to the principles of Vedanta and Yoga, emphasizing the idea of the essential unity of all beings, transcending religious and cultural differences.

Teachings and Philosophy

Vivekananda's teachings centred on the principles of Vedanta and the practice of Yoga, emphasizing the divinity of the soul, the oneness of existence, and the potential of human beings to attain spiritual enlightenment. He believed in the harmonious coexistence of science and religion, viewing them as complementary paths to understanding the ultimate reality. His philosophy was not confined to metaphysical ideas but extended to practical spirituality, where he encouraged individuals to serve society selflessly, upholding the idea of "Jiva is Shiva" – every human being is a manifestation of the divine.

He was also a strong advocate for education, considering it the key to social transformation. He believed that education should not only focus on intellectual development but also on character building and the realization of one's inner strength. For Vivekananda, the empowerment of the masses, especially women and the underprivileged, was essential for India's progress.

Contribution to Indian Nationalism and Social Reform

Swami Vivekananda is often hailed as a pioneer of Indian nationalism. His vision of India was rooted in a spiritual foundation, where religious unity would lead to social and political strength. He sought to awaken the Indian youth to their immense potential, urging them to embrace fearlessness, self-reliance, and moral integrity. His famous call, "Arise, awake, and stop not until the goal is reached," continues to resonate as a powerful message of self-empowerment and national pride.

Vivekananda was also a social reformer who criticized the rigid caste system, gender discrimination, and religious intolerance. He believed that India's rejuvenation would come through the upliftment of the downtrodden and the dismantling of oppressive social structures. His emphasis on karma yoga, or selfless service, laid the groundwork for future social and political movements in India, including the Indian independence struggle.

Establishment of the Ramakrishna Mission

In 1897, Vivekananda founded the Ramakrishna Mission, an organization dedicated to social service, education, and spiritual development. The Mission continues to operate schools, hospitals, and charitable institutions worldwide, reflecting Vivekananda's belief in the importance of combining spiritual knowledge with practical action. The Ramakrishna Mission remains a living embodiment of his philosophy of serving humanity as a path to self-realization.

Legacy and Influence

Swami Vivekananda passed away at the young age of 39 on July 4, 1902, but his legacy endures. His teachings have influenced a wide range of people, from political leaders like Mahatma Gandhi and Subhas Chandra Bose to spiritual teachers like Sri Aurobindo and Paramahansa Yogananda. In the West, his thoughts on Vedanta and Yoga shaped the intellectual discourse on spirituality, and he played a key role in the early spread of Indian spiritual practices to Europe and America.

His birthday, January 12, is celebrated as National Youth Day in India, in recognition of his enduring message to the younger generation. His words continue to inspire millions to strive for personal excellence, social justice, and spiritual enlightenment, making Swami Vivekananda a timeless figure in the global spiritual and cultural landscape.

Swami Vivekananda was much more than a spiritual leader; he was a visionary who laid the foundation for modern Indian thought, blending ancient wisdom with contemporary ideals. His emphasis on individual growth, social responsibility, and spiritual harmony continues to serve as a guiding light for generations. Through his life, teachings, and work, he not only revived the spiritual ethos of India but also gave the world a universal message of peace, unity, and compassion.

(Source : rkmath.org)

Contents

Preface

Since the dawn of history, various extraordinary phenomena have been recorded as happening amongst human beings. Witnesses are not wanting in modern times to attest to the fact of such events, even in societies living under the full blaze of modern science. The vast mass of such evidence is unreliable, as coming from ignorant, superstitious, or fraudulent persons. In many instances the so-called miracles are imitations. But what do they imitate? It is not the sign of a candid and scientific mind to throw overboard anything without proper investigation. Surface scientists, unable to explain the various extraordinary mental phenomena, strive to ignore their very existence. They are, therefore, more culpable than those who think that their prayers are answered by a being, or beings, above the clouds, or than those who believe that their petitions will make such beings change the course of the universe. The latter have the excuse of ignorance, or at least of a defective system of education, which has taught them dependence upon such beings, a dependence which has become a part of their degenerate nature. The former have no such excuse.

For thousands of years such phenomena have been studied, investigated, and generalised, the whole ground of the religious faculties of man has been analysed, and the practical result is the science of Râja-Yoga. Raja-Yoga does not, after the unpardonable manner of some modern scientists, deny the existence of facts which are difficult to explain; on the other hand, it gently yet in no uncertain terms tells the superstitious that miracles, and answers to prayers, and powers of faith, though true as facts, are not rendered comprehensible through the superstitious explanation of attributing them to the agency of a being, or beings, above the clouds. It declares that each man is only a conduit for the infinite ocean of knowledge and power that lies behind mankind. It teaches that desires and wants are in man, that the power of supply is also in man; and that wherever and whenever a desire, a want, a prayer has been fulfilled, it was out of this infinite magazine that the supply came, and not from any supernatural being. The idea of supernatural beings may rouse to a certain extent the power of action in man, but it also brings spiritual decay. It brings dependence; it brings fear; it brings superstition. It degenerates into a horrible belief in the natural weakness of man. There is no supernatural, says the Yogi, but there are in nature gross manifestations and subtle manifestations. The subtle are the causes, the gross the effects. The gross can be easily perceived by the senses; not so the subtle.

The practice of Raja-Yoga will lead to the acquisition of the more subtle perceptions.

All the orthodox systems of Indian philosophy have one goal in view, the liberation of the soul through perfection. The method is by Yoga. The word Yoga covers an immense ground, but both the Sânkhya and the Vedanta Schools point to Yoga in some form or other.

The subject of the present book is that form of Yoga known as Raja-Yoga. The aphorisms of Patanjali are the highest authority on Raja-Yoga, and form its textbook. The other philosophers, though occasionally differing from Patanjali in some philosophical points, have, as a rule, acceded to his method of practice a decided consent. The first part of this book comprises several lectures to classes delivered by the present writer in New York. The second part is a rather free translation of the aphorisms (Sutras) of Patanjali, with a running commentary. Effort has been made to avoid technicalities as far as possible, and to keep to the free and easy style of conversation. In the first part some simple and specific directions are given for the student who wants to practice, *but all such are especially and earnestly reminded that, with few exceptions, Yoga can only be safely learnt by direct contact with a teacher.* If these conversations succeed in awakening a desire for further information on the subject, the teacher will not be wanting.

The system of Patanjali is based upon the system of the Sankhyas, the points of difference being very few. The two most important differences are, first, that Patanjali admits a Personal God in the form of a first teacher, while the only God the Sankhyas admit is a nearly perfected being, temporarily in charge of a cycle of creation. Second, the Yogis hold the mind to be equally all-pervading with the soul, or Purusha, and the Sankhyas do not.

THE AUTHOR

CHAPTER I
Prayer

सतन्मयो ह्यमृत ईशसंस्थो ज्ञः सर्वगो भुवनस्यास्य गोप्ता।

य ईशेऽस्य जगतो नित्यमेव नान्यो हेतुर्विद्यत ईशनाय॥

यो ब्रह्माणं विदधाति पूर्व यो वै वेदांश्च प्रहिणोति तस्मै।

तं ह देवं आत्मबुध्दिप्रकाशं मुमुक्षुर्वै शरणमहं प्रपद्ये॥

"He is the Soul of the Universe; He is Immortal; His is the Rulership; He is the All-knowing, the All-pervading, the Protector of the Universe, the Eternal Ruler. None else is there efficient to govern the world eternally. He who at the beginning of creation projected Brahmâ (i.e. the universal consciousness), and who delivered the Vedas unto him — seeking liberation I go for refuge unto that effulgent One, whose light turns the understanding towards the Âtman."

Shvetâshvatara-Upanishad, VI. 17-18.

DEFINITION OF BHAKTI

Bhakti-Yoga is a real, genuine search after the Lord, a search beginning, continuing, and ending in love. One single moment of the madness of extreme love to God brings us eternal freedom. "Bhakti", says Nârada in his explanation of the Bhakti-aphorisms, "is intense love to God"; "When a man gets it, he loves all, hates none; he becomes satisfied for ever"; "This love cannot be reduced to any earthly benefit", because so long as worldly desires last, that kind of love does not come; "Bhakti is greater than karma, greater than Yoga, because these are intended for an object in view, while Bhakti is its own fruition, its own means and its own end."

Bhakti has been the one constant theme of our sages. Apart from the special writers on Bhakti, such as Shândilya or Narada, the great commentators on the *Vyâsa-Sutras*, evidently advocates of knowledge (Jnâna), have also something very suggestive to say about love. Even when the commentator is anxious to explain many, if not all, of the texts so as to make them import a sort of dry knowledge, the *Sutras*, in the chapter on worship especially, do not lend themselves to be easily manipulated in that fashion.

There is not really so much difference between knowledge (Jnana) and love (Bhakti) as people sometimes imagine. We shall see, as we go on, that in the end they converge and meet at the same point. So also is it with Râja-Yoga, which when pursued as a means to attain liberation, and not (as unfortunately it frequently becomes in the hands of charlatans and mystery-mongers) as an instrument to hoodwink the unwary, leads us also to the same goal.

The one great advantage of Bhakti is that it is the easiest and the most natural way to reach the great divine end in view; its great disadvantage is that in its lower forms it oftentimes degenerates into hideous fanaticism. The fanatical crew in Hinduism, or Mohammedanism, or Christianity, have always been almost exclusively recruited from these worshippers on the lower planes of Bhakti. That singleness of attachment (Nishthâ) to a loved object, without which no genuine love can grow, is very often also the cause of the denunciation of everything else. All the weak and undeveloped minds in every religion or country have only one way of loving their own ideal, i.e. by hating every other ideal. Herein is the explanation of why the same man who is so lovingly attached to his own ideal of God, so devoted to his own ideal of religion, becomes a howling fanatic as soon as he sees or hears anything of any other ideal. This kind of love is somewhat like the canine instinct of guarding the master's property from intrusion; only, the instinct of the dog is better than the reason of man, for the dog never mistakes its master for an enemy in whatever dress he may come before it. Again, the fanatic loses all power of judgment. Personal considerations are in his case of such absorbing interest that to him it is no question at all what a man says — whether it is right or wrong; but the one thing he is always particularly careful to know is who says it. The same man who is kind, good, honest, and loving to people of his own opinion, will not hesitate to do the vilest deeds when they are directed against persons beyond the pale of his own religious brotherhood.

But this danger exists only in that stage of Bhakti which is called the *preparatory* (Gauni). When Bhakti has become ripe and has passed into that form which is called the *supreme* (Parâ), no more is there any fear of these hideous manifestations of fanaticism; that soul which is overpowered by this higher form of Bhakti is too near the God of Love to become an instrument for the diffusion of hatred.

It is not given to all of us to be harmonious in the building up of our characters in this life: yet we know that that character is of the noblest type in which all these three — knowledge and love and Yoga — are harmoniously fused. Three things are necessary for a bird to fly — the two wings and the tail as a rudder for steering. Jnana (Knowledge) is the one wing, Bhakti (Love) is the other, and Yoga is the tail that keeps up the balance. For those who cannot pursue all these three forms of worship together in harmony and take up, therefore, Bhakti alone as their way, it is necessary always to remember that forms and ceremonials, though absolutely necessary for the progressive soul, have no other value than taking us on to that state in which we feel the most intense love to God.

There is a little difference in opinion between the teachers of knowledge and those of love, though both admit the power of Bhakti. The Jnanis hold Bhakti to be an instrument of liberation, the Bhaktas look upon it both as the instrument and the thing to be attained. To my mind this is a distinction without much difference. In fact, Bhakti, when used as an instrument, really means a lower form of worship, and the higher form becomes inseparable from the lower form of realisation at a later stage. Each seems to lay a great stress upon his own peculiar method of worship, forgetting that with perfect love true knowledge is bound to come even unsought, and that from perfect knowledge true love is inseparable.

Bearing this in mind let us try to understand what the great Vedantic commentators have to say on the subject. In explaining the Sutra Âvrittirasakridupadeshât (Meditation is necessary, that having been often enjoined.), Bhagavân Shankara says, "Thus people say, 'He is devoted to the king, he is devoted to the Guru'; they say this of him who follows his Guru, and does so, having that following as the one end in view. Similarly they say, 'The loving wife meditates on her loving husband'; here also a kind of eager and continuous remembrance is meant." This is devotion according to Shankara.

"Meditation again is a constant remembrance (of the thing meditated upon) flowing like an unbroken stream of oil poured out from one vessel to another. When this kind of remembering has been attained (in relation to God) all bondages break. Thus it is spoken of in the scriptures regarding constant remembering as a means to liberation. This remembering again is of the same form as seeing, because it is of the same meaning as in the passage, 'When He who is far and near is seen, the bonds of the heart are broken, all doubts vanish, and all effects of work disappear' He who is near can be seen, but he who is far can only be remembered. Nevertheless the scripture says that he have to see Him who is near as well as Him who, is far, thereby indicating to us that the above kind of *remembering* is as good as *seeing*. This remembrance when exalted assumes the same form as seeing.... Worship is constant remembering as may be seen from the essential texts of scriptures. Knowing, which is the same as repeated worship, has been described as constant remembering.... Thus the memory, which has attained to the height of what is as good as direct perception, is spoken of in the Shruti as a means of liberation. 'This Atman is not to be reached through various sciences, nor by intellect, nor by much study of the Vedas. Whomsoever this Atman desires, by him is the Atman attained, unto him this Atman discovers Himself.' Here, after saying that mere hearing, thinking and meditating are not the means of attaining this Atman, it is said, 'Whom this Atman desires, by him the Atman is attained.' The extremely beloved is desired; by whomsoever this Atman is extremely beloved, he becomes the most beloved of the Atman. So that this beloved may attain the Atman, the Lord Himself helps. For it has been said by the Lord: 'Those who are constantly attached to Me and worship Me with love — I give that direction to their will by which they come to Me.' Therefore it is said that, to whomsoever this remembering, which is of the same form as direct perception, is very dear, because it is dear to the Object of such memory perception, he is desired by the Supreme Atman, by him the Supreme Atman is attained. This constant remembrance is denoted by the word Bhakti." So says Bhagavân Râmânuja in his commentary on the Sutra Athâto Brahma-jijnâsâ (Hence follows a dissertation on Brahman.).

In commenting on the Sutra of Patanjali, Ishvara pranidhânâdvâ, i.e. "Or by the worship of the Supreme Lord" — Bhoja says, "Pranidhâna is that sort of Bhakti in which, without seeking results, such as sense-enjoyments etc., all works are dedicated to that Teacher of teachers." Bhagavan Vyâsa also, when commenting on the same, defines Pranidhana as "the form of Bhakti by which the mercy of the Supreme Lord comes to the Yogi, and blesses him by granting him his desires". According to Shândilya, "Bhakti is intense love to God." The best definition is, however, that given by the king of Bhaktas, Prahlâda:

या प्रीतिरविवेकानां विषयेष्वनपायिनी। त्वामनुस्मरतः सा मे हृदयान्मापसर्पतु॥

"That deathless love which the ignorant have for the fleeting objects of the senses — as I keep meditating on Thee — may not that love slip away from my heart!" *Love!* For whom? For the Supreme Lord Ishvara. Love for any other being, however great cannot be Bhakti; for, as Ramanuja says in his *Shri Bhâshya*, quoting an ancient Âchârya, i.e. a great teacher:

आब्रह्मस्तम्बपर्यन्ताः जगदन्तर्व्यवस्थिताः। प्राणिनः कर्मजनितसंसारवशवर्तिनः॥
यतस्ततो न ते ध्याने ध्यानिनामुपकारकाः। अविद्यान्तर्गतास्सर्वे ते हि संसारगोचराः॥

"From Brahmâ to a clump of grass, all things that live in the world are slaves of birth and death caused by Karma; therefore they cannot be helpful as objects of meditation, because they are all in ignorance and subject to change." In commenting on the word Anurakti used by Shandilya, the commentator Svapneshvara says that it means Anu, after, and Rakti, attachment; i.e. the attachment which comes after the knowledge of the nature and glory of God; else a blind attachment to any one, e.g. to wife or children, would be Bhakti. We plainly see, therefore, that Bhakti is a series or succession of mental efforts at religious realisation beginning with ordinary worship and ending in a supreme intensity of love for Ishvara.

CHAPTER II
The Philosophy of Ishvara

Who is Ishvara? Janmâdyasya yatah — "From whom is the birth, continuation, and dissolution of the universe," — He is Ishvara — "the Eternal, the Pure, the Ever-Free, the Almighty, the All-Knowing, the All-Merciful, the Teacher of all teachers"; and above all, Sa Ishvarah anirvachaniya-premasvarupah — "He the Lord is, of His own nature, inexpressible Love." These certainly are the definitions of a Personal God. Are there then two Gods — the "Not this, not this," the Sat-chit-ânanda, the Existence-Knowledge-Bliss of the philosopher, and this God of Love of the Bhakta? No, it is the same Sat-chit-ananda who is also the God of Love, the impersonal and personal in one. It has always to be understood that the Personal God worshipped by the Bhakta is not separate or different from the Brahman. All is Brahman, the One without a second; only the Brahman, as unity or absolute, is too much of an abstraction to be loved and worshipped; so the Bhakta chooses the relative aspect of Brahman, that is, Ishvara, the Supreme Ruler. To use a simile: Brahman is as the clay or substance out of which an infinite variety of articles are fashioned. As clay, they are all one; but form or manifestation differentiates them. Before every one of them was made, they all existed potentially in the clay, and, of course, they are identical substantially; but when formed, and so long as the form remains, they are separate and different; the clay-mouse can never become a clay-elephant, because, as manifestations, form alone makes them what they are, though as unformed clay they are all one. Ishvara is the highest manifestation of the Absolute Reality, or in other words, the highest possible reading of the Absolute by the human mind. Creation is eternal, and so also is Ishvara.

In the fourth Pâda of the fourth chapter of his *Sutras*, after stating the almost infinite power and knowledge which will come to the liberated soul after the attainment of Moksha, Vyâsa makes the remark, in an aphorism, that none, however, will get the power of creating, ruling, and dissolving the universe, because that belongs to God alone. In explaining the Sutra it is easy for the dualistic commentators to show how it is ever impossible for a subordinate soul, Jiva, to have the infinite power and total independence of God. The thorough dualistic commentator Madhvâchârya deals with this passage in his usual summary method by quoting a verse from the *Varâha Purâna*.

In explaining this aphorism the commentator Râmânuja says, "This doubt being raised, whether among the powers of the liberated souls is included that unique power of the Supreme One, that is, of creation etc. of the universe and even the Lordship of all, or whether, without that, the glory of the liberated consists only in the direct perception of the Supreme One, we get as an argument the following: It is reasonable that the liberated get the Lordship of the universe, because the scriptures say, 'He attains to extreme sameness with the Supreme One and all his desires are realised.' Now extreme sameness and realisation of all desires cannot be attained without the unique power of the Supreme Lord, namely, that of governing the universe. Therefore, to attain the realisation of all desires and the extreme sameness with the Supreme, we must all admit that the liberated get the power of ruling the whole universe. To this we reply, that the liberated get all the powers except that of ruling the universe. Ruling the universe is guiding the form and the life and the desires of all the sentient and the non-sentient beings. The liberated ones from whom all that veils His true nature has been removed, only enjoy the unobstructed perception of the Brahman, but do not possess the power of ruling the universe. This is proved from the scriptural text, "From whom all these things are born, by which all that are born live, unto whom they, departing, return — ask about it. That is Brahman.' If this quality of ruling the universe be a quality common even to the liberated then this text would not apply as a definition of Brahman defining Him through His rulership of the universe. The uncommon attributes alone define a thing; therefore in texts like —

'My beloved boy, alone, in the beginning there existed the One without a second. That saw and felt, "I will give birth to the many." That projected heat.' — 'Brahman indeed alone existed in the beginning. That One evolved. That projected a blessed form, the Kshatra. All these gods are Kshatras: Varuna, Soma, Rudra, Parjanya, Yama, Mrityu, Ishâna.' — 'Atman indeed existed alone in the beginning; nothing else vibrated; He thought of projecting the world; He projected the world after.' — 'Alone Nârâyana existed; neither Brahmâ, nor Ishana, nor the Dyâvâ-Prithivi, nor the stars, nor water, nor fire, nor Soma, nor the sun. He did not take pleasure alone. He after His meditation had one daughter, the ten organs, etc.' — and in others as, 'Who living in the earth is separate from the earth, who living in the Atman, etc.' — the Shrutis speak of the Supreme One as the subject of the work of ruling the universe. . . . Nor in these descriptions of the ruling of the universe is there any position for the liberated soul, by which such a soul may have the ruling of the universe ascribed to it."

In explaining the next Sutra, Ramanuja says, "If you say it is not so, because there are direct texts in the Vedas in evidence to the contrary, these texts refer to the glory of the liberated in the spheres of the subordinate deities." This also is an easy solution of the difficulty. Although the system of Ramanuja admits the unity of the total, within that totality of existence there are, according to him, eternal differences. Therefore, for all practical purposes, this system also being dualistic, it was easy for Ramanuja to keep the distinction between the personal soul and the Personal God very clear.

We shall now try to understand what the great representative of the Advaita School has to say on the point. We shall see how the Advaita system maintains all the hopes and aspirations of the dualist intact, and at the same time propounds its own solution of the problem in consonance with the high destiny of divine humanity. Those who aspire to retain their individual mind even after liberation and to remain distinct will have ample opportunity of realising their aspirations and enjoying the blessing of the qualified Brahman. These are they who have been spoken of in the *Bhâgavata Purâna* thus: "O king, such are the, glorious qualities of the Lord that the sages whose only pleasure is in the Self, and from whom all fetters have fallen off, even they love the Omnipresent with the love that is for love's sake." These are they who are spoken of by the Sânkhyas as getting merged in nature in this cycle, so that, after attaining perfection, they may come out in the next as lords of world-systems. But none of these ever becomes equal to God (Ishvara). Those who attain to that state where there is neither creation, nor created, nor creator, where there is neither knower, nor knowable, nor knowledge, where there is neither *I*, nor *thou*, nor *he*, where there is neither subject, nor object, nor relation, "there, who is seen by whom?" — such persons have gone beyond everything to "where words cannot go nor mind", gone to that which the Shrutis declare as "Not this, not this"; but for those who cannot, or will not reach this state, there will inevitably remain the triune vision of the one undifferentiated Brahman as

nature, soul, and the interpenetrating sustainer of both
— Ishvara. So, when Prahlâda forgot himself, he found
neither the universe nor its cause; all was to him one
Infinite, undifferentiated by name and form; but as soon
as he remembered that he was Prahlada, there was the
universe before him and with it the Lord of the universe
— "the Repository of an infinite number of blessed
qualities". So it was with the blessed Gopis. So long as
they had lost sense of their own personal identity and
individuality, they were all Krishnas, and when they began
again to think of Him as the One to be worshipped, then
they were Gopis again, and immediately

तासामाविरभूच्छौरि: स्मयमानमुखाम्बुज:।
पीताम्बरधर: स्रग्वी साक्षान्मन्मथमन्मथ:॥

(*Bhagavata*) — "Unto them appeared Krishna with a
smile on His lotus face, clad in yellow robes and having
garlands on, the embodied conqueror (in beauty) of the
god of love."

Now to go back to our Acharya Shankara: "Those",
he says, "who by worshipping the qualified Brahman
attain conjunction with the Supreme Ruler, preserving
their own mind — is their glory limited or unlimited?
This doubt arising, we get as an argument: Their glory
should be unlimited because of the scriptural texts, 'They
attain their own kingdom', 'To him all the gods offer
worship', 'Their desires are fulfilled in all the worlds'. As
an answer to this, Vyasa writes, 'Without the power of
ruling the universe.' Barring the power of creation etc.

of the universe, the other powers such as Animâ etc. are acquired by the liberated. As to ruling the universe, that belongs to the eternally perfect Ishvara. Why? Because He is the subject of all the scriptural texts as regards creation etc., and the liberated souls are not mentioned therein in any connection whatsoever. The Supreme Lord indeed is alone engaged in ruling the universe. The texts as to creation etc. all point to Him. Besides, there is given the adjective 'ever-perfect'. Also the scriptures say that the powers Anima etc. of the others are from the search after and the worship of God. Therefore they have no place in the ruling of the universe. Again, on account of their possessing their own minds, it is possible that their wills may differ, and that, whilst one desires creation, another may desire destruction. The only way of avoiding this conflict is to make all wills subordinate to some one will. Therefore the conclusion is that the wills of the lib erated are dependent on the will of the Supreme Ruler."

Bhakti, then, can be directed towards Brahman, only in His personal aspect. क्लेशोऽधिकतरस्तेषामव्यक्तासक्तचेतसाम् — "The way is more difficult for those whose mind is attached to the Absolute!" Bhakti has to float on smoothly with the current of our nature. True it is that we cannot have; any idea of the Brahman which is not anthropomorphic, but is it not equally true of everything we know? The greatest psychologist the world has ever known, Bhagavan Kapila, demonstrated ages ago that human consciousness is one of the elements in the make-up of all the objects of our perception and conception, internal as well as external.

Beginning with our bodies and going up to Ishvara, we may see that every object of our perception is this consciousness plus something else, whatever that may be; and this unavoidable mixture is what we ordinarily think of as reality. Indeed it is, and ever will be, all of the reality that is possible for the human mind to know. Therefore to say that Ishvara is unreal, because He is anthropomorphic, is sheer nonsense. It sounds very much like the occidentals squabble on idealism and realism, which fearful-looking quarrel has for its foundation a mere play on the word "real". The idea of Ishvara covers all the ground ever denoted and connoted by the word real, and Ishvara is as real as anything else in the universe; and after all, the word real means nothing more than what has now been pointed out. Such is our philosophical conception of Ishvara.

CHAPTER III

Spiritual Realisation, the Aim of Bhakti-Yoga

To the Bhakta these dry details are necessary only to strengthen his will; beyond that they are of no use to him. For he is treading on a path which is fitted very soon to lead him beyond the hazy and turbulent regions of reason, to lead him to the realm of realisation. He, soon, through the mercy of the Lord, reaches a plane where pedantic and powerless reason is left far behind, and the mere intellectual groping through the dark gives place to the daylight of direct perception. He no more reasons and believes, he almost perceives. He no more argues, he senses. And is not this seeing God, and feeling God, and enjoying God higher than everything else? Nay, Bhaktas have not been wanting who have maintained that it is higher than even Moksha — liberation. And is it not also the highest utility? There are people — and a good many of them too — in the world who are convinced that only that is of use and utility which brings to man creature-comforts. Even religion, God, eternity, soul, none of these is of any use to them, as they do not bring them money or physical comfort. To such, all those things which do not go to gratify the senses and appease the appetites are of no utility. In every mind, utility, however, is conditioned by its own peculiar wants. To men, therefore, who never rise higher than eating, drinking, begetting progeny, and dying, the only gain is in sense enjoyments; and they must wait and go through many more births and reincarnations to learn to feel even the faintest necessity for anything higher. But those to whom the eternal interests of the soul are of much higher value than the fleeting interests of this mundane life, to whom the gratification of the senses is but like the thoughtless play of the baby, to them God and the love of God form the highest and the only utility of human existence. Thank God there are some such still living in this world of too much worldliness.

Bhakti-Yoga, as we have said, is divided into the Gauni or the preparatory, and the Parâ or the supreme forms. We shall find, as we go on, how in the preparatory stage we unavoidably stand in need of many concrete helps to enable us to get on; and indeed the mythological and symbological parts of all religions are natural growths which early environ the aspiring soul and help it Godward. It is also a significant fact that spiritual giants have been produced only in those systems of religion where there is an exuberant growth of rich mythology and ritualism. The dry fanatical forms of religion which attempt to eradicate all that is poetical, all that is beautiful and sublime, all that gives a firm grasp to the infant mind tottering in its Godward way — the forms which attempt to break down the very ridge-poles of the spiritual roof, and in their ignorant and superstitious conceptions of truth try to drive away all that is life-giving, all that furnishes the formative material to the spiritual plant growing in the human soul — such forms of religion too soon find that all that is left to them is but an empty shell, a contentless frame of words and sophistry with perhaps a little flavour of a kind of social scavengering or the so-called spirit of reform.

The vast mass of those whose religion is like this, are conscious or unconscious materialists — the end and aim of their lives here and hereafter being enjoyment, which indeed is to them the alpha and the omega of human life, and which is their Ishtâpurta; work like street-cleaning and scavengering, intended for the material comfort of man is, according to them, the be-all and end-all of human existence; and the sooner the followers of this curious mixture of ignorance and fanaticism come out in their true colours and join, as they well deserve to do, the ranks of atheists and materialists, the better will it be for the world. One ounce of the practice of righteousness and of spiritual Self-realisation outweighs tons and tons of frothy talk and nonsensical sentiments. Show us one, but one gigantic spiritual genius growing out of all this dry dust of ignorance and fanaticism; and if you cannot, close your mouths, open the windows of your hearts to the clear light of truth, and sit like children at the feet of those who know what they are talking about — the sages of India. Let us then listen attentively to what they say.

CHAPTER IV
The Need of Guru

Every soul is destined to be perfect, and every being, in the end, will attain the state of perfection. Whatever we are now is the result of our acts and thoughts in the past; and whatever we shall be in the future will be the result of what we think end do now. But this, the shaping of our own destinies, does not preclude our receiving help from outside; nay, in the vast majority of cases such help is absolutely necessary. When it comes, the higher powers and possibilities of the soul are quickened, spiritual life is awakened, growth is animated, and man becomes holy and perfect in the end.

This quickening impulse cannot be derived from books. The soul can only receive impulses from another soul, and from nothing else. We may study books all our lives, we may become very intellectual, but in the end we find that we have not developed at all spiritually. It is not true that a high order of intellectual development always goes hand in hand with a proportionate development of the spiritual side in Man. In studying books we are sometimes deluded into thinking that thereby we are being spiritually helped; but if we analyse the effect of the study of books on ourselves, we shall find that at the utmost it is only our intellect that derives profit from such studies, and not our inner spirit. This inadequacy of books to quicken spiritual growth is the reason why, although almost every one of us can *speak* most wonderfully on spiritual matters, when it comes to action and the living of a truly spiritual life, we find ourselves so awfully deficient. To quicken the spirit, the impulse must come from another soul.

The person from whose soul such impulse comes is called the Guru — the teacher; and the person to whose soul the impulse is conveyed is called the Shishya — the student. To convey such an impulse to any soul, in the first place, the soul from which it proceeds must possess the power of transmitting it, as it were, to another; and in the second place, the soul to which it is transmitted must be fit to receive it. The seed must be a living seed, and the field must be ready ploughed; and when both these conditions are fulfilled, a wonderful growth of genuine religion takes place. "The true preacher of religion has to be of wonderful capabilities, and clever shall his hearer be" — आश्चर्यो वक्ता कुशलोऽस्य लब्धा; and when both of these are really wonderful and extraordinary, then will a splendid spiritual awakening result, and not otherwise. Such alone are the real teachers, and such alone are also the real students, the real aspirants. All others are only playing with spirituality. They have just a little curiosity awakened, just a little intellectual aspiration kindled in them, but are merely standing on the outward fringe of the horizon of religion. There is no doubt some value even in that, as it may in course of time result in the awakening of a real thirst for religion; and it is a mysterious law of nature that as soon as the field is ready, the seed *must* and does come; as soon as the soul earnestly desires to have religion, the transmitter of the religious force *must* and does appear to help that soul. When the power that attracts the light of religion in the receiving soul is full and strong, the power which answers to that attraction and sends in light does come as a matter of course.

There are, however, certain great dangers in the way. There is, for instance, the danger to the receiving soul of its mistaking momentary emotions for real religious yearning. We may study that in ourselves. Many a time in our lives, somebody dies whom we loved; we receive a blow; we feel that the world is slipping between our fingers, that we want something surer and higher, and that we must become religious. In a few days that wave of feeling has passed away, and we are left stranded just where we were before. We are all of us often mistaking such impulses for real thirst after religion; but as long as these momentary emotions are thus mistaken, that continuous, real craving of the soul for religion will not come, and we shall not find the true transmitter of spirituality into our nature. So whenever we are tempted to complain of our search after the truth that we desire so much, proving vain, instead of so complaining, our first duty ought to be to look into our own souls and find whether the craving in the heart is real.

Then in the vast majority of cases it would be discovered that we were not fit for receiving the truth, that there was no real thirst for spirituality.

There are still greater dangers in regard to the *transmitter*, the Guru. There are many who, though immersed in ignorance, yet, in the pride of their hearts, fancy they know everything, and not only do not stop there, but offer to take others on their shoulders; and thus the blind leading the blind, both fall into the ditch.

अविद्यायामन्तरे वर्तमानाः स्वयं
धीराः पण्डितम्मन्यमानाः ।
दन्द्रम्यमाणाः परियन्ति मूढा
अन्धेनैव नीयमाना यथान्धाः ॥

— "Fools dwelling in darkness, wise in their own conceit, and puffed up with vain knowledge, go round and round staggering to and fro, like blind men led by the blind." — (Katha Up., I. ii. 5). The world is full of these. Every one wants to be a teacher, every beggar wants to make a gift of a million dollars! Just as these beggars are ridiculous, so are these teachers.

CHAPTER V

Qualifications of the Aspirant and the Teacher

How are we to know a teacher, then? The sun requires no torch to make him visible, we need not light a candle in order to see him. When the sun rises, we instinctively become aware of the fact, and when a teacher of men comes to help us, the soul will instinctively know that truth has already begun to shine upon it. Truth stands on its own evidence, it does not require any other testimony to prove it true, it is self effulgent. It penetrates into the innermost corners of our nature, and in its presence the whole universe stands up and says, "This is truth." The teachers whose wisdom and truth shine like the light of the sun are the very greatest the world has known, and they are worshipped as God by the major portion of mankind. But we may get help from comparatively lesser ones also; only we ourselves do not possess intuition enough to judge properly of the man from whom we receive teaching and guidance; so there ought to be certain tests, certain conditions, for the teacher to satisfy, as there are also for the taught.

The conditions necessary for the taught are purity, a real thirst after knowledge, and perseverance. No impure soul can be really religious. Purity in thought, speech, and act is absolutely necessary for any one to be religious. As to the thirst after knowledge, it is an old law that we all get whatever we want. None of us can get anything other than what we fix our hearts upon. To pant for religion truly is a very difficult thing, not at all so easy as we generally imagine. Hearing religious talks or reading religious books is no proof yet of a real want felt in the heart; there must be a continuous struggle, a constant fight, an unremitting grappling with our lower nature, till the higher want is actually felt and the victory is achieved. It is not a question of one or two days, of years, or of lives; the struggle may have to go on for hundreds of lifetimes. The success sometimes may come immediately, but we must be ready to wait patiently even for what may look like an infinite length of time. The student who sets out with such a spirit of perseverance will surely find success and realisation at last.

In regard to the teacher, we must see that he knows the spirit of the scriptures. The whole world reads Bibles, Vedas, and Korans; but they are all only words, syntax, etymology, philology, the dry bones of religion. The teacher who deals too much in words and allows the mind to be carried away by the force of words loses the spirit. It is the knowledge of the *spirit* of the scriptures alone that constitutes the true religious teacher. The network of the words of the scriptures is like a huge forest in which the human mind often loses itself and finds no way out. शब्दजालं महारण्यं चित्तभ्रमणकारणम्। — "The network of words is a big forest; it is the cause of a curious wandering of the mind." "The various methods of joining words, the various methods of speaking in beautiful language, the various methods of explaining the diction of the scriptures are only for the disputations and enjoyment of the learned, they do not conduce to the development of spiritual perception" - वाग्वैश्वरी शब्दझरी शास्त्रव्याख्यानकौशलम् । वैदुष्यं विदुषां तद्वद् भुक्तये न तु मुक्तये ॥ Those who employ such methods to impart religion to others are only desirous to show off their learning, so that the world may praise them as great scholars. You will find that no one of the great teachers of the world ever went into these various explanations of the text; there is with them no attempt at "text-torturing", no eternal playing upon the meaning of words and their roots. Yet they nobly taught, while others who have nothing to teach have taken up a word sometimes and written a three-volume book on its origin, on the man who used it first, and on what that man was accustomed to eat, and how long he slept, and so on.

Bhagavân Ramakrishna used to tell a story of some men who went into a mango orchard and busied themselves in counting the leaves, the twigs, and the branches, examining their colour, comparing their size, and noting down everything most carefully, and then got up a learned discussion on each of these topics, which were undoubtedly highly interesting to them. But one of them, more sensible than the others, did not care for all these things. and instead thereof, began to eat the mango fruit. And was he not wise? So leave this counting of leaves and twigs and note-taking to others. This kind of work has its proper place, but not here in the spiritual domain. You never see a strong spiritual man among these "leaf counters". Religion, the highest aim, the highest glory of man, does not require so much labour. If you want to be a Bhakta, it is not at all necessary for you to know whether Krishna was born in Mathurâ or in Vraja, what he was doing, or just the exact date on which he pronounced the teachings of the Gitâ. You only require to *feel* the craving for the beautiful lessons of duty and love in the Gita. All the other particulars about it and its author are for the enjoyment of the learned. Let them have what they desire. Say "Shântih, Shântih" to their learned controversies, and let *us* "eat the mangoes".

The second condition necessary in the teacher is — sinlessness. The question is often asked, "Why should we look into the character and personality of a teacher? We have only to judge of what he says, and take that up." This is not right. If a man wants to teach me something of dynamics, or chemistry, or any other physical science, he may be anything he likes, because what the physical sciences require is merely an intellectual equipment; but in the spiritual sciences it is impossible from first to last that there can be any spiritual light in the soul that is impure. What religion can an impure man teach? The *sine qua non* of acquiring spiritual truth for one's self or for imparting it to others is the purity of heart and soul. A vision of God or a glimpse of the beyond never comes until the soul is pure. Hence with the teacher of religion we must see first what he *is*, and then what he says. He must be perfectly pure, and then alone comes the value of his words, because he is only then the true "transmitter". What can he transmit if he has not spiritual power in himself? There must be the worthy vibration of spirituality in the mind of the teacher, so that it may be sympathetically conveyed to the mind of the taught. The function of the teacher is indeed an affair of the transference of something, and not one of mere stimulation of the existing intellectual or other faculties in the taught. Something real and appreciable as an influence comes from the teacher and goes to the taught. Therefore the teacher must be pure.

The third condition is in regard to the motive. The teacher must not teach with any ulterior selfish motive — for money, name, or fame; his work must be simply out of love, out of pure love for mankind at large. The only medium through which spiritual force can be transmitted is love. Any selfish motive, such as the desire for gain or for name, will immediately destroy this conveying median. God is love, and only he who has known God as love can be a teacher of godliness and God to man.

When you see that in your teacher these conditions are all fulfilled, you are safe; if they are not, it is unsafe to allow yourself to be taught by him, for there is the great danger that, if he cannot convey goodness to your heart, he may convey wickedness. This danger must by all means be guarded against. श्रोत्रियोऽवृजिनोऽकामहतो यो ब्रह्मवित्तमः — "He who is learned in the scriptures, sinless, unpolluted by lust, and is the greatest knower of the Brahman" is the real teacher.

From what has been said, it naturally follows that we cannot be taught to love, appreciate, and assimilate religion everywhere and by everybody. The "books in the running brooks, sermons in stones, and good in everything" is all very true as a poetical figure: but nothing can impart to a man a single grain of truth unless he has the undeveloped germs of it in himself. To whom do the stones and brooks preach sermons? To the human soul, the lotus of whose inner holy shrine is already quick with life. And the light which causes the beautiful opening out of this lotus comes always from the good and wise teacher. When the heart has thus been opened, it becomes fit to receive teaching from the stones or the brooks, the stars, or the sun, or the moon, or from any thing which has its existence in our divine universe; but the unopened heart will see in them nothing but mere stones or mere brooks. A blind man may go to a museum, but he will not profit by it in any way; his eyes must be opened first, and then alone he will be able to learn what the things in the museum can teach.

This eye-opener of the aspirant after religion is the teacher. With the teacher, therefore, our relationship is the same as that between an ancestor and his descendant. Without faith, humility, submission, and veneration in our hearts towards our religious teacher, there cannot be any growth of religion in us; and it is a significant fact that, where this kind of relation between the teacher and the taught prevails, there alone gigantic spiritual men are growing; while in those countries which have neglected to keep up this kind of relation the religious teacher has become a mere lecturer, the teacher expecting his five dollars and the person taught expecting his brain to be filled with the teacher's words, and each going his own way after this much has been done. Under such circumstances spirituality becomes almost an unknown quantity. There is none to transmit it and none to have it transmitted to. Religion with such people becomes business; they think they can obtain it with their dollars. Would to God that religion could be obtained so easily! But unfortunately it cannot be.

Religion, which is the highest knowledge and the highest wisdom, cannot be bought, nor can it be acquired from books. You may thrust your head into all the corners of the world, you may explore the Himalayas, the Alps, and the Caucasus, you may sound the bottom of the sea and pry into every nook of Tibet and the desert of Gobi, you will not find it anywhere until your heart is ready for receiving it and your teacher has come. And when that divinely appointed teacher comes, serve him with childlike confidence and simplicity, freely open your heart to his influence, and see in him God manifested. Those who come to seek truth with such a spirit of love and veneration, to them the Lord of Truth reveals the most wonderful things regarding truth, goodness, and beauty.

CHAPTER VI
Incarnate Teachers and Incarnation

Wherever His name is spoken, that very place is holy. How much more so is the man who speaks His name, and with what veneration ought we to approach that man out of whom comes to us spiritual truth! Such great teachers of spiritual truth are indeed very few in number in this world, but the world is never altogether without them. They are always the fairest flowers of human life — अहेतुकदयासिन्धुः — "the ocean of mercy without any motive". आचार्यं मां विजानीयात् — "Know the Guru to be Me", says Shri Krishna in the *Bhagavata*. The moment the world is absolutely bereft of these, it becomes a hideous hell and hastens on to its destruction.

Higher and nobler than all ordinary ones are another set of teachers, the Avatâras of Ishvara, in the world. They can transmit spirituality with a touch, even with a mere wish. The lowest and the most degraded characters become in one second saints at their command. They are the Teachers of all teachers, the highest manifestations of

God through man. We cannot see God except through them. We cannot help worshipping them; and indeed they are the only ones whom we are bound to worship.

No man can really see God except through these human manifestations. If we try to see God otherwise, we make for ourselves a hideous caricature of Him and believe the caricature to be no worse than the original. There is a story of an ignorant man who was asked to make an image of the God Shiva, and who, after days of hard struggle, manufactured only the image of a monkey. So whenever we try to think of God as He is in His absolute perfection, we invariably meet with the most miserable failure, because as long as we are men, we cannot conceive Him as anything higher than man. The time will come when we shall transcend our human nature and know Him as He is; but as long as we are men, we must worship Him in man and as man. Talk as you may, try as you may, you cannot think of God except as a man. You may deliver great intellectual discourses on God and on all things under the sun, become great rationalists and prove to your satisfaction that all these accounts of the Avataras of God as man are nonsense. But let us come for a moment to practical common sense. What is there behind this kind of remarkable intellect? Zero, nothing, simply so much froth. When next you hear a man delivering a great intellectual lecture against this worship of the Avataras of God, get hold of him and ask what *his* idea of God is, what *he* understands by "omnipotence", "omnipresence", and all similar terms, beyond the spelling of the words.

He really means nothing by them; he cannot formulate as their meaning any idea unaffected by his own human nature; he is no better off in this matter than the man in the street who has not read a single book. That man in the street, however, is quiet and does not disturb the peace of the world, while this big talker creates disturbance and misery among mankind. Religion is, after all, realisation, and we must make the sharpest distinction between talk; and intuitive experience. What we experience in the depths of our souls is realisation. Nothing indeed is so uncommon as common sense in regard to this matter.

By our present constitution we are limited and bound to see God as man. If, for instance the buffaloes want to worship God, they will, in keeping with their own nature, see Him as a huge buffalo; if a fish wants to worship God, it will have to form an Idea of Him as a big fish, and man has to think of Him as man. And these various conceptions are not due to morbidly active imagination. Man, the buffalo, and the fish all may be supposed to represent so many different vessels, so to say. All these vessels go to the sea of God to get filled with water, each according to its own shape and capacity; in the man the water takes the shape of man, in the buffalo, the shape of a buffalo and in the fish, the shape of a fish. In each of these vessels there is the same water of the sea of God. When men see Him, they see Him as man, and the animals, if they have any conception of God at all, must see Him as animal each according to its own ideal. So we cannot help seeing God as man, and, therefore, we are bound to worship Him as man. There is no other way.

Two kinds of men do not worship God as man — the human brute who has no religion, and the Paramahamsa who has risen beyond all the weaknesses of humanity and has transcended the limits of his own human nature. To him all nature has become his own Self. He alone can worship God as He is. Here, too, as in all other cases, the two extremes meet. The extreme of ignorance and the other extreme of knowledge — neither of these go through acts of worship. The human brute does not worship because of his ignorance, and the Jivanmuktas (free souls) do not worship because they have realised God in themselves. Being between these two poles of existence, if any one tells you that he is not going to worship God as man, take kindly care of that man; he is, not to use any harsher term, an irresponsible talker; his religion is for unsound and empty brains.

God understands human failings and becomes man to do good to humanity:

यदा यदा हि धर्मस्य ग्लानिर्भवति भारत। अभ्युत्थानमधर्मस्य तदात्मानं सृजाम्यहम्॥
परित्राणाय साधूनां विनाशाय च दुष्कृताम्। धर्मसंस्थापनार्थाय सम्भवामि युगे युगे॥

— "Whenever virtue subsides and wickedness prevails, I manifest Myself. To establish virtue, to destroy evil, to save the good I come from Yuga (age) to Yuga."

अवजानन्ति मां मूढा मानुषीं तनुमाश्रितम्।
परं भावमजानन्तो मम भूतमहेश्वरम्॥

— "Fools deride Me who have assumed the human form, without knowing My real nature as the Lord of the universe." Such is Shri Krishna's declaration in the Gita on Incarnation. "When a huge tidal wave comes," says Bhagavan Shri Ramakrishna, "all the little brooks and ditches become full to the brim without any effort or consciousness on their own part; so when an Incarnation comes, a tidal wave of spirituality breaks upon the world, and people feel spirituality almost full in the air."

CHAPTER VII
The Mantra: Om: Word and Wisdom

But we are now considering not these Mahâ-purushas, the great Incarnations, but only the Siddha-Gurus (teachers who have attained the goal); they, as a rule, have to convey the germs of spiritual wisdom to the disciple by means of words (Mantras) to be meditated upon. What are these Mantras? The whole of this universe has, according to Indian philosophy, both name and form (Nâma-Rupa) as its conditions of manifestation. In the human microcosm, there cannot be a single wave in the mind-stuff (Chittavritti) unconditioned by name and form. If it be true that nature is built throughout on the same plan, this kind of conditioning by name and form must also be the plan of the building of the whole of the cosmos. यथा एकेन मृत्पिण्डेन सर्वं मृन्मयं विज्ञातं स्यात् — "As one lump of clay being known, all things of clay are known", so the knowledge of the microcosm must lead to the knowledge of the macrocosm. Now form is the outer crust, of which the name or the idea is the inner essence or kernel. The body is the form, and the mind or the Antahkarana is the name, and sound-symbols are universally associated with Nâma (name) in all beings having the power of speech. In the individual man the thought-waves rising in the limited Mahat or Chitta (mind-stuff), must manifest themselves, first as *words*, and then as the more concrete *forms*.

In the universe, Brahmâ or Hiranyagarbha or the cosmic Mahat first manifested himself as name, and then as form, i.e. as this universe. All this expressed sensible universe is the form, behind which stands the eternal inexpressible Sphota, the manifester as *Logos* or Word. This eternal Sphota, the essential eternal material of all ideas or names is the power through which the Lord creates the universe, nay, the Lord first becomes conditioned as the Sphota, and then evolves Himself out as the yet more concrete sensible universe. This Sphota has one word as its only possible symbol, and this is the ओं (Om). And as by no possible means of analysis can we separate the word from the idea this Om and the eternal Sphota are inseparable; and therefore, it is out of this holiest of all holy words, the mother of all names and forms, the eternal Om, that the whole universe may be supposed to have been created. But it may be said that, although thought and word are inseparable, yet as there may be various word-symbols for the same thought, it is not necessary that this particular word Om should be the word representative of the thought, out of which the universe has become manifested. To this objection we reply that this Om is the only possible symbol which covers the whole ground, and there is none other like it. The Sphota is the material of all words, yet it is not any definite word in its fully formed state. That is to say, if all the peculiarities which distinguish one word from another be removed, then what remains will be the Sphota; therefore this Sphota is called the Nâda-Brahma. the *Sound-Brahman.*

Now, as every word-symbol, intended to express the inexpressible Sphota, will so particularise it that it will no longer be the Sphota, that symbol which particularises it the least and at the same time most approximately expresses its nature, will be the truest symbol thereof; and this is the Om, and the Om only; because these three letters अ उ म (A.U.M.), pronounced in combination as Om, may well be the generalised symbol of all possible sounds. The letter A is the least differentiated of all sounds, therefore Krishna says in the Gita अक्षराणां अकारोऽस्मि— "I am A among the letters". Again, all articulate sounds are produced in the space within the mouth beginning with the root of the tongue and ending in the lips — the throat sound is A, and M is the last lip sound, and the U exactly represents the rolling forward of the impulse which begins at the root of the tongue till it ends in the lips. If properly pronounced, this Om will represent the whole phenomenon of sound-production, and no other word can do this; and this, therefore, is the fittest symbol of the Sphota, which is the real meaning of the Om. And as the symbol can never be separated from the thing signified, the Om and the Sphota are one. And as the Sphota, being the finer side of the manifested universe, is nearer to God and is indeed that first manifestation of divine wisdom this Om is truly symbolic of God. Again, just as the "One only" Brahman, the Akhanda-Sachchidânanda, the undivided Existence-Knowledge-Bliss, can be conceived by imperfect human souls only from particular standpoints and associated with particular qualities, so this universe, His body, has also to be thought of along the line of the thinker's mind.

This direction of the worshipper's mind is guided by its prevailing elements or Tattvas. The result is that the same God will be seen in various manifestations as the possessor of various predominant qualities, and the same universe will appear as full of manifold forms. Even as in the case of the least differentiated and the most universal symbol Om, thought and sound-symbol are seen to be inseparably associated with each other, so also this law of their inseparable association applies to the many differentiated views of God and the universe: each of them therefore must have a particular word-symbol to express it. These word-symbols, evolved out of the deepest spiritual perception of sages, symbolise and express, as nearly as possible the particular view of God and the universe they stand for. And as the Om represents the Akhanda, the undifferentiated Brahman, the others represent the Khanda or the differentiated views of the same Being; and they are all helpful to divine meditation and the acquisition of true knowledge.

CHAPTER VIII
Worship of Substitutes and Images

The next points to be considered are the worship of Pratikas or of things more or less satisfactory as substitutes for God, and the worship of Pratimâs or images. What is the worship of God through a Pratika? It is अब्रह्मणि ब्रह्मदृष्ट्याऽनुसन्धानम् — Joining the mind with devotion to that which is not Brahman, taking it to be Brahman" — says Bhagavân Râmânuja. "Worship the mind as Brahman this is internal; and the Âkâsha as Brahman, this is with regard to the Devas", says Shankara. The mind is an internal Pratika, the Akasha is an external one, and both have to be worshipped as substitutes of God. He continues, "Similarly — 'the Sun is Brahman, this is the command', 'He who worships Name as Brahman' — in all such passages the doubt arises as to the worship of Pratikas." The word Pratika means going towards; and worshipping a Pratika is worshipping something as a substitute which is, in some one or more respects, like Brahman more and more, but is not Brahman. Along with the Pratikas mentioned in the Shrutis there are various others to be found in the Purânas and the Tantras. In this kind of Pratika-worship may be included all the various forms of Pitri-worship and Deva-worship.

Now worshipping Ishvara and Him alone is Bhakti; the worship of anything else — Deva, or Pitri, or any other being — cannot be Bhakti. The various kinds of worship of the various Devas are all to be included in ritualistic Karma, which gives to the worshipper only a particular result in the form of some celestial enjoyment, but can neither give rise to Bhakti nor lead to Mukti. One thing, therefore, has to be carefully borne in mind. If, as it may happen in some cases, the highly philosophic ideal, the supreme Brahman, is dragged down by Pratika-worship to the level of the Pratika, and the Pratika itself is taken to be the Atman of the worshipper or his Antaryâmin (Inner Ruler), the worshipper gets entirely misled, as no Pratika can really be the Atman of the worshipper.

But where Brahman Himself is the object of worship, and the Pratika stands only as a substitute or a suggestion thereof, that is to say, where, through the Pratika the omnipresent Brahman is worshipped — the Pratika itself being idealised into the cause of all, Brahman — the worship is positively beneficial; nay, it is absolutely necessary for all mankind until they have all got beyond the primary or preparatory state of the mind in regard to worship. When, therefore, any gods or other beings are worshipped in and for themselves, such worship is only a ritualistic Karma; and as a Vidyâ (science) it gives us only the fruit belonging to that particular Vidya; but when the Devas or any other beings are looked upon as Brahman and worshipped, the result obtained is the same as by the worshipping of Ishvara. This explains how, in many cases, both in the Shrutis and the Smritis, a god, or a sage, or some other extraordinary being is taken up and lifted, as it were, out of his own nature and idealised into Brahman, and is then worshipped. Says the Advaitin, "Is not everything Brahman when the name and the form have been removed from it?" "Is not He, the Lord, the innermost Self of every one?" says the Vishishtâdvaitin. फलम् आदित्याद्युपासनेषु ब्रह्मैव दास्यति सर्वाध्यक्षत्वात् — "The fruition of even the worship of Adityas etc. Brahman Himself bestows, because He is the Ruler of all." Says Shankara in his *Brahma-Sutra-Bhâsya* — ईदृशं चात्र ब्रह्मण उपास्यत्वं यतः प्रतीकेषु तत्दृष्ट्याध्यारोपणं प्रतिमादिषु इव विष्णुवादीनाम्। "Here in this way does Brahman become the object of worship, because He, as Brahman, is superimposed on the Pratikas, just as Vishnu etc. are superimposed upon images etc."

The same ideas apply to the worship of the Pratimas as to that of the Pratikas; that is to say, if the image stands for a god or a saint, the worship is not the result of Bhakti, and does not lead lo liberation; but if it stands for the one God, the worship thereof will bring both Bhakti and Mukti. Of the principal religions of the world we see Vedantism, Buddhism, and certain forms of Christianity freely using images; only two religions, Mohammedanism and Protestantism, refuse such help. Yet the Mohammedans use the grave of their saints and martyrs almost in the place of images; and the Protestants, in rejecting all concrete helps to religion, are drifting away every year farther and farther from spirituality till at present there is scarcely any difference between the advanced Protestants and the followers of August Comte, or agnostics who preach ethics alone. Again, in Christianity and Mohammedanism whatever exists of image worship is made to fall under that category in which the Pratika or the Pratima is worshipped in itself, but not as a "help to the vision" (Drishtisaukaryam) of God; therefore it is at best only of the nature of ritualistic Karmas and cannot produce either Bhakti or Mukti. In this form of image-worship, the allegiance of the soul is given to other things than Ishvara, and, therefore, such use of images, or graves, or temples, or tombs, is real idolatry; it is in itself neither sinful nor wicked — it is a rite — a Karma, and worshippers must and will get the fruit thereof.

CHAPTER IX
The Chosen Ideal

The next thing to be considered is what we know as Ishta-Nishthâ. One who aspires to be a Bhakta must know that "so many opinions are so many ways". He must know that all the various sects of the various religions are the various manifestations of the glory of the same Lord. "They call You by so many names; they divide You, as it were, by different names, yet in each one of these is to be found Your omnipotence....You reach the worshipper through all of these, neither is there any special time so long as the soul has intense love for You. You are so easy of approach; it is my misfortune that I cannot love You." Not only this, the Bhakta must take care not to hate, nor even to criticise those radiant sons of light who are the founders of various sects; he must not even hear them spoken ill of. Very few indeed are those who are at once the possessors of an extensive sympathy and power of appreciation, as well as an intensity of love. We find, as a rule, that liberal and sympathetic sects lose the intensity of religious feeling, and in their hands, religion is apt to degenerate into a kind of politico-social club life. On the other hand, intensely narrow sectaries, whilst displaying a very commendable love of their own ideals, are seen to have acquired every particle of that love by hating every one who is not of exactly the same opinions as themselves. Would to God that this world was full of men who were as intense in their love as worldwide in their sympathies! But such are only few and far between. Yet we know that it is practicable to educate large numbers of human beings into the ideal of a wonderful blending of both the width and the intensity of love; and the way to do that is by this path of the Istha-Nishtha or "steadfast devotion to the chosen ideal". Every sect of every religion presents only one ideal of its own to mankind, but the eternal Vedantic religion opens to mankind an infinite number of doors for ingress into the inner shrine of divinity, and places before humanity an almost inexhaustible array of ideals, there being in each of them a manifestation of the Eternal One. With the kindest solicitude, the Vedanta points out to aspiring men and women the numerous roads, hewn out of the solid rock of the realities of human life, by the glorious sons, or human manifestations, of God, in the past and in the present, and stands with outstretched arms to welcome all — to welcome even those that are yet to be — to that Home of Truth and that Ocean of Bliss, wherein the human soul, liberated from the net of Mâyâ, may transport itself with perfect freedom and with eternal joy.

Bhakti-Yoga, therefore, lays on us the imperative command not to hate or deny any one of the various paths that lead to salvation. Yet the growing plant must be hedged round to protect it until it has grown into a tree. The tender plant of spirituality will die if exposed too early to the action of a constant change of ideas and ideals. Many people, in the name of what may be called religious liberalism, may be seen feeding their idle curiosity with a continuous succession of different ideals. With them, hearing new things grows into a kind of disease, a sort of religious drink-mania. They want to hear new things just by way of getting a temporary nervous excitement, and when one such exciting influence has had its effect on them, they are ready for another. Religion is with these people a sort of intellectual opium-eating, and there it ends. "There is another sort of man", says Bhagavan Ramakrishna, "who is like the pearl-oyster of the story. The pearl-oyster leaves its bed at the bottom of the sea, and comes up to the surface to catch the rain-water when the star Svâti is in the ascendant. It floats about on the surface of the sea with its shell wide open, until it has succeeded in catching a drop of the rain-water, and then it dives deep down to its sea-bed, and there rests until it has succeeded in fashioning a beautiful pearl out of that rain-drop."

This is indeed the most poetical and forcible way in which the theory of Ishta-Nishtha has ever been put. This Eka-Nishtha or devotion to one ideal is absolutely necessary for the beginner in the practice of religious devotion. He must say with Hanuman in the Râmâyana, "Though I know that the Lord of Shri and the Lord of Jânaki are both manifestations of the same Supreme Being, yet my all in all is the lotus-eyed Râma." Or, as was said by the sage Tulasidâsa, he must say, "Take the sweetness of all, sit with all, take the name of all, say yea, yea, but keep your seat firm." Then, if the devotional aspirant is sincere, out of this little seed will come a gigantic tree like the Indian banyan, sending out branch after branch and root after root to all sides, till it covers the entire field of religion. Thus will the true devotee realise that He who was his own ideal in life is worshipped in all ideals by all sects, under all names, and through all forms.

CHAPTER X
The Method and
the Means

In regard to the method and the means of Bhakti-Yoga we read in the commentary of Bhagavan Ramanuja on the *Vedanta-Sutras*: "The attaining of That comes through discrimination, controlling the passions, practice, sacrificial work, purity, strength, and suppression of excessive joy." Viveka or discrimination is, according to Ramanuja, discriminating, among other things, the pure food from the impure. According to him, food becomes impure from three causes: (1) by the nature of the food itself, as in the case of garlic etc.; (2) owing to its coming from wicked and accursed persons; and (3) from physical impurities, such as dirt, or hair, etc. The Shrutis say, When the food is pure, the Sattva element gets purified, and the memory becomes unwavering", and Ramanuja quotes this from the Chhândogya Upanishad.

The question of food has always been one of the most vital with the Bhaktas. Apart from the extravagance into which some of the Bhakti sects have run, there is a great truth underlying this question of food. We must remember that, according to the Sankhya philosophy, the Sattva, Rajas, and Tamas, which in the state of homogeneous equilibrium form the Prakriti, and in the heterogeneous disturbed condition form the universe — are both the substance and the quality of Prakriti. As such they are the materials out of which every human form has been manufactured, and the predominance of the Sattva material is what is absolutely necessary for spiritual development. The materials which we receive through our food into our body-structure go a great way to determine our mental constitution; therefore the food we eat has to be particularly taken care of. However, in this matter, as in others, the fanaticism into which the disciples invariably fall is not to be laid at the door of the masters.

And this discrimination of food is, after all, of secondary importance. The very same passage quoted above is explained by Shankara in his Bhâshya on the Upanishads in a different way by giving an entirely different meaning to the word Âhâra, translated generally as food. According to him, "That which is gathered in is Ahara. The knowledge of the sensations, such as sound etc., is gathered in for the enjoyment of the enjoyer (self); the purification of the knowledge which gathers in the perception of the senses is the purifying of the food (Ahara). The word 'purification-of-food' means the acquiring of the knowledge of sensations untouched by the defects of attachment, aversion, and delusion; such is the meaning. Therefore such knowledge or Ahara

being purified, the Sattva material of the possessor it —
the internal organ — will become purified, and the Sattva
being purified, an unbroken memory of the Infinite One,
who has been known in His real nature from scriptures,
will result."

These two explanations are apparently conflicting,
yet both are true and necessary. The manipulating and
controlling of what may be called the finer body, viz the
mood, are no doubt higher functions than the controlling
of the grosser body of flesh. But the control of the
grosser is absolutely necessary to enable one to arrive at
the control of the finer. The beginner, therefore, must
pay particular attention to all such dietetic rules as have
come down from the line of his accredited teachers; but
the extravagant, meaningless fanaticism, which has driven
religion entirely to the kitchen, as may be noticed in the
case of many of our sects, without any hope of the noble
truth of that religion ever coming out to the sunlight
of spirituality, is a peculiar sort of pure and simple
materialism. It is neither Jnâna, nor Bhakti, nor Karma;
it is a special kind of lunacy, and those who pin their
souls to it are more likely to go to lunatic asylums than
to Brahmaloka. So it stands to reason that discrimination
in the choice of food is necessary for the attainment of
this higher state of mental composition which cannot be
easily obtained otherwise.

Controlling the passions is the next thing to be attended
to. To restrain the Indriyas (organs) from going towards

the objects of the senses, to control them and bring them under the guidance of the will, is the very central virtue in religious culture. Then comes the practice of self-restraint and self-denial. All the immense possibilities of divine realisation in the soul cannot get actualised without struggle and without such practice on the part of the aspiring devotee. "The mind must always think of the Lord." It is very hard at first to compel the mind to think of the Lord always, but with every new effort the power to do so grows stronger in us. "By practice, O son of Kunti, and by non-attachment is it attained", says Shri Krishna in the Gita. And then as to sacrificial work, it is understood that the five great sacrificed (To gods, sages, manes, guests, and all creatures.) (Panchamahâyajna) have to be performed as usual.

Purity is absolutely the basic work, the bed-rock upon which the whole Bhakti-building rests. Cleansing the external body and discriminating the food are both easy, but without internal cleanliness and purity, these external observances are of no value whatsoever. In the list of qualities conducive to purity, as given by Ramanuja, there are enumerated, Satya, truthfulness; Ârjava, sincerity; Dayâ, doing good to others without any gain to one's self; Ahimsâ, not injuring others by thought, word, or deed; Anabhidhyâ, not coveting others' goods, not thinking vain thoughts, and not brooding over injuries received from another. In this list, the one idea that deserves special notice is Ahimsa, non-injury to others. This duty of non-injury is, so to speak, obligatory on us in relation to all beings. As with some, it does not simply mean the non-injuring of human beings and mercilessness towards the lower animals; nor, as with some others, does it mean the protecting of cats and dogs and feeding of ants with sugar — with liberty to injure brother-man in every horrible way! It is remarkable that almost every good idea in this world can be carried to a disgusting extreme. A good practice carried to an extreme and worked in accordance with the letter of the law becomes a positive evil. The stinking monks of certain religious sects, who do not bathe lest the vermin on their bodies should be killed, never think of the discomfort and disease they bring to their fellow human beings. They do not, however, belong to the religion of the Vedas!

The test of Ahimsa is absence of jealousy. Any man may do a good deed or make a good gift on the spur of the moment or under the pressure of some superstition or priestcraft; but the real lover of mankind is he who is jealous of none. The so-called great men of the world may all be seen to become jealous of each other for a small name, for a little fame, and for a few bits of gold. So long as this jealousy exists in a heart, it is far away from the perfection of Ahimsa. The cow does not eat meat, nor does the sheep. Are they great Yogis, great non-injurers (Ahimsakas)? Any fool may abstain from eating this or that; surely that gives him no more distinction than to herbivorous animals. The man who will mercilessly cheat widows and orphans and do the vilest deeds for money is worse than any brute even if he lives entirely on grass.

The man whose heart never cherishes even the thought of injury to any one, who rejoices at the prosperity of even his greatest enemy, that man is the Bhakta, he is the Yogi, he is the Guru of all, even though he lives every day of his life on the flesh of swine. Therefore we must always remember that external practices have value only as helps to develop internal purity. It is better to have internal purity alone when minute attention to external observances is not practicable. But woe unto the man and woe unto the nation that forgets the real, internal, spiritual essentials of religion and mechanically clutches with death-like grasp at all external forms and never lets them go. The forms have value only so far as they are expressions of the life within. If they have ceased to express life, crush them out without mercy.

The next means to the attainment of Bhakti-Yoga is strength (Anavasâda). "This Atman is not to be attained by the weak", says the Shruti. Both physical weakness and mental weakness are meant here. "The strong, the hardy" are the only fit students. What can puny, little, decrepit things do? They will break to pieces whenever the mysterious forces of the body and mind are even slightly awakened by the practice of any of the Yogas. It is "the young, the healthy, the strong" that can score success. Physical strength, therefore, is absolutely necessary. It is the strong body alone that can bear the shock of reaction resulting from the attempt to control the organs. He who wants to become a Bhakta must be strong, must be healthy. When the miserably weak attempt any of the Yogas, they are likely to get some incurable malady, or they weaken their minds. Voluntarily weakening the body is really no prescription for spiritual enlightenment.

The mentally weak also cannot succeed in attaining the Atman. The person who aspires to be a Bhakta must be cheerful. In the Western world the idea of a religious man is that he never smiles, that a dark cloud must always hang over his face, which, again, must be long drawn with the jaws almost collapsed. People with emaciated bodies and long faces are fit subjects for the physician, they are not Yogis. It is the cheerful mind that is persevering. It is the strong mind that hews its way through a thousand difficulties. And this, the hardest task of all, the cutting of our way out of the net of Maya, is the work reserved only for giant wills.

Yet at the same time excessive mirth should be avoided (Anuddharsha). Excessive mirth makes us unfit for serious thought. It also fritters away the energies of the mind in vain. The stronger the will, the less the yielding to the sway of the emotions. Excessive hilarity is quite as objectionable as too much of sad seriousness, and all religious realisation is possible only when the mind is in a steady, peaceful condition of harmonious equilibrium.

It is thus that one may begin to learn how to love the Lord.

Raja-Yoga

Each soul is potentially divine.

The goal is to manifest this Divinity within by controlling nature, external and internal.

Do this either by work, or worship, or psychic control, or philosophy — by one, or more, or all of these — and be free.

This is the whole of religion. Doctrines, or dogmas, or rituals, or books, or temples, or forms, are but secondary details.

CHAPTER I
Introductory

All our knowledge is based upon experience. What we call inferential knowledge, in which we go from the less to the more general, or from the general to the particular, has experience as its basis. In what are called the exact sciences, people easily find the truth, because it appeals to the particular experiences of every human being. The scientist does not tell you to believe in anything, but he has certain results which come from his own experiences, and reasoning on them when he asks us to believe in his conclusions, he appeals to some universal experience of humanity. In every exact science there is a basis which is common to all humanity, so that we can at once see the truth or the fallacy of the conclusions drawn therefrom. Now, the question is: Has religion any such basis or not? I shall have to answer the question both in the affirmative and in the negative.

Religion, as it is generally taught all over the world, is said to be based upon faith and belief, and, in most cases, consists only of different sets of theories, and that is the reason why we find all religions quarrelling with one another. These theories, again, are based upon belief. One man says there is a great Being sitting above the clouds and governing the whole universe, and he asks me to believe that solely on the authority of his assertion. In the same way, I may have my own ideas, which I am asking others to believe, and if they ask a reason, I cannot give them any. This is why religion and metaphysical philosophy have a bad name nowadays. Every educated man seems to say, "Oh, these religions are only bundles of theories without any standard to judge them by, each man preaching his own pet ideas." Nevertheless, there is a basis of universal belief in religion, governing all the different theories and all the varying ideas of different sects in different countries. Going to their basis we find that they also are based upon universal experiences.

In the first place, if you analyse all the various religions of the world, you will find that these are divided into two classes, those with a book and those without a book. Those with a book are the strongest, and have the largest number of followers. Those without books have mostly died out, and the few new ones have very small following. Yet, in all of them we find one consensus of opinion, that the truths they teach are the results of the experiences of particular persons. The Christian asks you to believe in his religion, to believe in Christ and to believe in him as the incarnation of God, to believe in a God, in a soul, and in a better state of that soul. If I ask him for reason, he says he believes in them. But if you go to the fountain-head of Christianity, you will find that it is based upon experience. Christ said he saw God; the disciples said they felt God; and so forth. Similarly, in Buddhism, it is Buddha's experience. He experienced certain truths, saw them, came in contact with them, and preached them to the world. So with the Hindus. In their books the writers, who are called Rishis, or sages, declare they experienced certain truths, and these they preach. Thus it is clear that all the religions of the world have been built upon that one universal and adamantine foundation of all our knowledge — direct experience. The teachers all saw God; they all saw their own souls, they saw their future, they saw their eternity, and what they saw they preached. Only there is this difference that by most of these religions especially in modern times, a peculiar claim is made, namely, that these experiences are impossible at the present day; they were only possible with a few men, who were the first founders of the religions that subsequently bore their names. At the present time these experiences have become obsolete, and, therefore, we have now to take religion on belief. This I entirely deny. If there has been one experience in this world in any particular branch of knowledge, it absolutely follows that that experience has been possible millions of times before, and will be repeated eternally. Uniformity is the rigorous law of nature; what once happened can happen always.

The teachers of the science of Yoga, therefore, declare that religion is not only based upon the experience of ancient times, but that no man can be religious until he has the same perceptions himself. Yoga is the science which teaches us how to get these perceptions. It is not much use to talk about religion until one has felt it. Why is there so much disturbance, so much fighting and quarrelling in the name of God? There has been more bloodshed in the name of God than for any other cause, because people never went to the fountain-head; they were content only to give a mental assent to the customs of their forefathers, and wanted others to do the same. What right has a man to say he has a soul if he does not feel it, or that there is a God if he does not see Him? If there is a God we must see Him, if there is a soul we must perceive it; otherwise it is better not to believe. It is better to be an outspoken atheist than a hypocrite. The modern idea, on the one hand, with the "learned" is that religion and metaphysics and all search after a Supreme Being are futile; on the other hand, with the semi-educated, the idea seems to be that these things really have no basis; their only value consists in the fact that they furnish strong motive powers for doing good to the world. If men believe in a God, they may become good, and moral, and so make good citizens. We cannot blame them for holding such ideas, seeing that all the teaching these men get is simply to believe in an eternal rigmarole of words, without any substance behind them. They are asked to live upon words; can they do it? If they could, I should not have the least regard for human nature. Man wants truth, wants to experience truth for himself; when he has grasped it, realised it, felt it within his heart of hearts, then alone, declare the Vedas, would all doubts vanish, all darkness be scattered, and all crookedness be made straight. "Ye children of immortality, even those who live in the highest sphere, the way is found; there is a way out of all this darkness, and that is by perceiving Him who is beyond all darkness; there is no other way."

The science of Râja-Yoga proposes to put before humanity a practical and scientifically worked out method of reaching this truth. In the first place, every science must have its own method of investigation. If you want to become an astronomer and sit down and cry "Astronomy! Astronomy!" it will never come to you. The same with chemistry. A certain method must be followed. You must go to a laboratory, take different substances, mix them up, compound them, experiment with them, and out of that will come a knowledge of chemistry. If you want to be an astronomer, you must go to an observatory, take a telescope, study the stars and planets, and then you will become an astronomer. Each science must have its own methods. I could preach you thousands of sermons, but they would not make you religious, until you practiced the method. These are the truths of the sages of all countries, of all ages, of men pure and unselfish, who had no motive but to do good to the world. They all declare that they have found some truth higher than what the senses can bring to us, and they invite verification. They ask us to take up the method and practice honestly, and then, if we do not find this higher truth, we will have the right to say there is no truth in the claim, but before we have done that, we are not rational in denying the truth of their assertions. So we must work faithfully using the prescribed methods, and light will come.

In acquiring knowledge we make use of generalisations, and generalisation is based upon observation. We first observe facts, then generalise, and then draw conclusions or principles. The knowledge of the mind, of the internal nature of man, of thought, can never be had until we have first the power of observing the facts that are going on within. It is comparatively easy to observe facts in the external world, for many instruments have been invented for the purpose, but in the internal world we have no instrument to help us. Yet we know we must observe in order to have a real science. Without a proper analysis, any science will be hopeless — mere theorising. And that is why all the psychologists have been quarrelling among themselves since the beginning of time, except those few who found out the means of observation.

The science of Raja-Yoga, in the first place, proposes to give us such a means of observing the internal states. The instrument is the mind itself. The power of attention, when properly guided, and directed towards the internal world, will analyse the mind, and illumine facts for us. The powers of the mind are like rays of light dissipated; when they are concentrated, they illumine. This is our only means of knowledge. Everyone is using it, both in the external and the internal world; but, for the psychologist, the same minute observation has to be directed to the internal world, which the scientific man directs to the external; and this requires a great deal of practice. From our childhood upwards we have been taught only to pay attention to things external, but never to things internal; hence most of us have nearly lost the faculty of observing the internal mechanism. To turn the mind as it were, inside, stop it from going outside, and then to concentrate all its powers, and throw them upon the mind itself, in order that it may know its own nature, analyse itself, is very hard work. Yet that is the only way to anything which will be a scientific approach to the subject.

What is the use of such knowledge? In the first place, knowledge itself is the highest reward of knowledge, and secondly, there is also utility in it. It will take away all our misery. When by analysing his own mind, man comes face to face, as it were, with something which is never destroyed, something which is, by its own nature, eternally pure and perfect, he will no more be miserable, no more unhappy. All misery comes from fear, from unsatisfied desire. Man will find that he never dies, and then he will have no more fear of death. When he knows that he is perfect, he will have no more vain desires, and both these causes being absent, there will be no more misery — there will be perfect bliss, even while in this body.

There is only one method by which to attain this knowledge, that which is called concentration. The chemist in his laboratory concentrates all the energies of his mind into one focus, and throws them upon the materials he is analysing, and so finds out their secrets. The astronomer concentrates all the energies of his mind and projects them through his telescope upon the skies; and the stars, the sun, and the moon, give up their secrets to him. The more I can concentrate my thoughts on the matter on which I am talking to you, the more light I can throw upon you. You are listening to me, and the more you concentrate your thoughts, the more clearly you will grasp what I have to say.

How has all the knowledge in the world been gained but by the concentration of the powers of the mind? The world is ready to give up its secrets if we only know how to knock, how to give it the necessary blow. The strength and force of the blow come through concentration. There is no limit to the power of the human mind. The more concentrated it is, the more power is brought to bear on one point; that is the secret.

It is easy to concentrate the mind on external things, the mind naturally goes outwards; but not so in the case of religion, or psychology, or metaphysics, where the subject and the object, are one. The object is internal, the mind itself is the object, and it is necessary to study the mind itself — mind studying mind. We know that there is the power of the mind called reflection. I am talking to you. At the same time I am standing aside, as it were, a second person, and knowing and hearing what I am talking. You work and think at the same time, while a portion of your mind stands by and sees what you are thinking. The powers of the mind should be concentrated and turned back upon itself, and as the darkest places reveal their secrets before the penetrating rays of the sun, so will this concentrated mind penetrate its own innermost secrets. Thus will we come to the basis of belief, the real genuine religion. We will perceive for ourselves whether we have souls, whether life is of five minutes or of eternity, whether there is a God in the universe or more. It will all be revealed to us. This is what Raja-Yoga proposes to teach. The goal of all its teaching is how to concentrate the minds, then, how to discover the innermost recesses of our own minds, then, how to generalise their contents and form our own conclusions from them. It, therefore, never asks the question what our religion is, whether we are Deists or Atheists, whether Christians, Jews, or Buddhists. We are human beings; that is sufficient. Every human being has the right and the power to seek for religion. Every human being has the right to ask the reason, why, and to have his question answered by himself, if he only takes the trouble.

So far, then, we see that in the study of this Raja-Yoga no faith or belief is necessary. Believe nothing until you find it out for yourself; that is what it teaches us. Truth requires no prop to make it stand. Do you mean to say that the facts of our awakened state require any dreams or imaginings to prove them? Certainly not. This study of Raja-Yoga takes a long time and constant practice. A part of this practice is physical, but in the main it is mental. As we proceed we shall find how intimately the mind is connected with the body. If we believe that the mind is simply a finer part of the body, and that mind acts upon the body, then it stands to reason that the body must react upon the mind. If the body is sick, the mind becomes sick also. If the body is healthy, the mind remains healthy and strong. When one is angry, the mind becomes disturbed. Similarly when the mind is disturbed, the body also becomes disturbed. With the majority of mankind the mind is greatly under the control of the body, their mind being very little developed. The vast mass of humanity is very little removed from the animals. Not only so, but in many instances, the power of control in them is little higher than that of the lower animals. We have very little command of our minds. Therefore to bring that command about, to get that control over body and mind, we must take certain physical helps. When the body is sufficiently controlled, we can attempt the manipulation of the mind. By manipulating the mind, we shall be able to bring it under our control, make it work as we like, and compel it to concentrate its powers as we desire.

According to the Raja-Yogi, the external world is but the gross form of the internal, or subtle. The finer is always the cause, the grosser the effect. So the external world is the effect, the internal the cause. In the same way external forces are simply the grosser parts, of which the internal forces are the finer. The man who has discovered and learned how to manipulate the internal forces will get the whole of nature under his control. The Yogi proposes to himself no less a task than to master the whole universe, to control the whole of nature. He wants to arrive at the point where what we call "nature's laws" will have no influence over him, where he will be able to get beyond them all. He will be master of the whole of nature, internal and external. The progress and civilisation of the human race simply mean controlling this nature.

Different races take to different processes of controlling nature. Just as in the same society some individuals want to control the external nature, and others the internal, so, among races, some want to control the external nature, and others the internal. Some say that by controlling internal nature we control everything. Others that by controlling external nature we control everything. Carried to the extreme both are right, because in nature there is no such division as internal or external. These are fictitious limitations that never existed. The externalists and the internalists are destined to meet at the same point, when both reach the extreme of their knowledge. Just as a physicist, when he pushes his knowledge to its limits, finds it melting away into metaphysics, so a metaphysician will find that what he calls mind and matter are but apparent distinctions, the reality being One.

The end and aim of all science is to find the unity, the One out of which the manifold is being manufactured, that One existing as many. Raja-Yoga proposes to start from the internal world, to study internal nature, and through that, control the whole — both internal and external. It is a very old attempt. India has been its special stronghold, but it was also attempted by other nations. In Western countries it was regarded as mysticism and people who wanted to practice it were either burned or killed as witches and sorcerers. In India, for various reasons, it fell into the hands of persons who destroyed ninety per cent of the knowledge, and tried to make a great secret of the remainder. In modern times many so-called teachers have arisen in the West worse than those of India, because the latter knew something, while these modern exponents know nothing.

Anything that is secret and mysterious in these systems of Yoga should be at once rejected. The best guide in life is strength. In religion, as in all other matters, discard everything that weakens you, have nothing to do with it. Mystery-mongering weakens the human brain. It has well-nigh destroyed Yoga — one of the grandest of sciences. From the time it was discovered, more than four thousand years ago, Yoga was perfectly delineated, formulated, and preached in India. It is a striking fact that the more modern the commentator the greater the mistakes he makes, while the more ancient the writer the more rational he is. Most of the modern writers talk of all sorts of mystery. Thus Yoga fell into the hands of a few persons who made it a secret, instead of letting the full blaze of daylight and reason fall upon it. They did so that they might have the powers to themselves.

In the first place, there is no mystery in what I teach. What little I know I will tell you. So far as I can reason it out I will do so, but as to what I do not know I will simply tell you what the books say. It is wrong to believe blindly. You must exercise your own reason and judgment; you must practice, and see whether these things happen or not. Just as you would take up any other science, exactly in the same manner you should take up this science for study. There is neither mystery nor danger in it. So far as it is true, it ought to be preached in the public streets, in broad daylight. Any attempt to mystify these things is productive of great danger.

Before proceeding further, I will tell you a little of the Sânkhya philosophy, upon which the whole of Raja-Yoga is based. According to the Sankhya philosophy, the genesis of perception is as follows: the affections of external objects are carried by the outer instruments to their respective brain centres or organs, the organs carry the affections to the mind, the mind to the determinative faculty, from this the Purusha (the soul) receives them, when perception results. Next he gives the order back, as it were, to the motor centres to do the needful. With the exception of the Purusha all of these are material, but the mind is much finer matter than the external instruments. That material of which the mind is composed goes also to form the subtle matter called the Tanmâtras. These become gross and make the external matter. That is the psychology of the Sankhya. So that between the intellect and the grosser matter outside there is only a difference in degree. The Purusha is the only thing which is immaterial. The mind is an instrument, as it were, in the hands of the soul, through which the soul catches external objects. The mind is constantly changing and vacillating, and can, when perfected, either attach itself to several organs, to one, or to none. For instance, if I hear the clock with great attention, I will not, perhaps, see anything although my eyes may be open, showing that the mind was not attached to the seeing organ, while it was to the hearing organ. But the perfected mind can be attached to all the organs simultaneously. It has the reflexive power of looking back into its own depths. This reflexive power is what the Yogi wants to attain; by concentrating the powers of the mind, and turning them inward, he seeks to know what is happening inside. There is in this no question of mere belief; it is the analysis arrived at by certain philosophers. Modern physiologists tell us that the eyes are not the organ of vision, but that the organ is in one of the nerve centres of the brain, and so with all the senses; they also tell us that these centres are formed of the same material as the brain itself. The Sankhyas also tell us the same thing. The former is a statement on the physical side, and the latter on the psychological side; yet both are the same. Our field of research lies beyond this.

The Yogi proposes to attain that fine state of perception in which he can perceive all the different mental states. There must be mental perception of all of them. One can perceive how the sensation is travelling, how the mind is receiving it, how it is going to the determinative faculty, and how this gives it to the Purusha. As each science requires certain preparations and has its own method, which must be followed before it could be understood, even so in Raja-Yoga.

Certain regulations as to food are necessary; we must use that food which brings us the purest mind. If you go into a menagerie, you will find this demonstrated at once. You see the elephants, huge animals, but calm and gentle; and if you go towards the cages of the lions and tigers, you find them restless, showing how much difference has been made by food. All the forces that are working in this body have been produced out of food; we see that every day. If you begin to fast, first your body will get weak, the physical forces will suffer; then after a few days, the mental forces will suffer also. First, memory will fail. Then comes a point, when you are not able to think, much less to pursue any course of reasoning. We have, therefore, to take care what sort of food we eat at the beginning, and when we have got strength enough, when our practice is well advanced, we need not be so careful in this respect. While the plant is growing it must be hedged round, lest it be injured; but when it becomes a tree, the hedges are taken away. It is strong enough to withstand all assaults.

A Yogi must avoid the two extremes of luxury and austerity. He must not fast, nor torture his flesh. He who does so, says the Gita, cannot be a Yogi: He who fasts, he who keeps awake, he who sleeps much, he who works too much, he who does no work, none of these can be a Yogi (Gita, VI, 16).

CHAPTER II
The First Steps

Râja-Yoga is divided into eight steps. The first is Yama — non-killing, truthfulness, non-stealing, continence, and non-receiving of any gifts. Next is Niyama — cleanliness, contentment, austerity, study, and self-surrender to God. Then comes Âsana, or posture; Prânâyâma, or control of Prâna; Pratyâhâra, or restraint of the senses from their objects; Dhâranâ, or fixing the mind on a spot; Dhyâna, or meditation; and Samâdhi, or superconsciousness. The Yama and Niyama, as we see, are moral trainings; without these as the basis no practice of Yoga will succeed. As these two become established, the Yogi will begin to realise the fruits of his practice; without these it will never bear fruit. A Yogi must not think of injuring anyone, by thought, word, or deed. Mercy shall not be for men alone, but shall go beyond, and embrace the whole world.

The next step is Asana, posture. A series of exercises, physical and mental, is to be gone through every day, until certain higher states are reached. Therefore it is quite necessary that we should find a posture in which we can remain long. That posture which is the easiest for one should be the one chosen. For thinking, a certain posture may be very easy for one man, while to another it may be very difficult. We will find later on that during the study of these psychological matters a good deal of activity goes on in the body. Nerve currents will have to be displaced and given a new channel. New sorts of vibrations will begin, the whole constitution will be remodelled as it were. But the main part of the activity will lie along the spinal column, so that the one thing necessary for the posture is to hold the spinal column free, sitting erect, holding the three parts — the chest, neck, and head — in a straight line. Let the whole weight of the body be supported by the ribs, and then you have an easy natural postures with the spine straight. You will easily see that you cannot think very high thoughts with the chest in. This portion of the Yoga is a little similar to the Hatha-Yoga which deals entirely with the physical body, its aim being to make the physical body very strong. We have nothing to do with it here, because its practices are very difficult, and cannot be learned in a day, and, after all, do not lead to much spiritual growth. Many of these practices you will find in Delsarte and other teachers, such as placing the body in different postures, but the object in these is physical, not psychological. There is not one muscle in the body over which a man cannot establish a perfect control. The heart can be made to stop or go on at his bidding, and each part of the organism can be similarly controlled.

The result of this branch of Yoga is to make men live long; health is the chief idea, the one goal of the Hatha-Yogi. He is determined not to fall sick, and he never does. He lives long; a hundred years is nothing to him; he is quite young and fresh when he is 150, without one hair turned grey. But that is all. A banyan tree lives sometimes 5000 years, but it is a banyan tree and nothing more. So, if a man lives long, he is only a healthy animal. One or two ordinary lessons of the Hatha-Yogis are very useful. For instance, some of you will find it a good thing for headaches to drink cold water through the nose as soon as you get up in the morning; the whole day your brain will be nice and cool, and you will never catch cold. It is very easy to do; put your nose into the water, draw it up through the nostrils and make a pump action in the throat.

After one has learned to have a firm erect seat, one has to perform, according to certain schools, a practice called the purifying of the nerves. This part has been rejected by some as not belonging to Raja-Yoga, but as so great an authority as the commentator Shankarâchârya advises it, I think fit that it should be mentioned, and I will quote his own directions from his commentary on the Shvetâshvatara Upanishad: "The mind whose dross has been cleared away by Pranayama, becomes fixed in Brahman; therefore Pranayama is declared. First the nerves are to be purified, then comes the power to practice Pranayama. Stopping the right nostril with the thumb, through the left nostril fill in air, according to capacity; then, without any interval, throw the air out through the right nostril, closing the left one. Again inhaling through the right nostril eject through the left, according to capacity; practicing this three or five times at four hours of the day, before dawn, during midday, in the evening, and at midnight, in fifteen days or a month purity of the nerves is attained; then begins Pranayama."

Practice is absolutely necessary. You may sit down and listen to me by the hour every day, but if you do not practice, you will not get one step further. It all depends on practice. We never understand these things until we experience them. We will have to see and feel them for ourselves. Simply listening to explanations and theories will not do. There are several obstructions to practice. The first obstruction is an unhealthy body: if the body is not in a fit state, the practice will be obstructed. Therefore we have to keep the body in good health; we have to take care of what we eat and drink, and what we do. Always use a mental effort, what is usually called "Christian Science," to keep the body strong. That is all — nothing further of the body. We must not forget that health is only a means to an end. If health were the end, we would be like animals; animals rarely become unhealthy.

The second obstruction is doubt; we always feel doubtful about things we do not see. Man cannot live upon words, however he may try. So, doubt comes to us as to whether there is any truth in these things or not; even the best of us will doubt sometimes. With practice, within a few days, a little glimpse will come, enough to give one encouragement and hope. As a certain commentator on Yoga philosophy says, "When one proof is obtained, however little that may be, it will give us faith in the whole teaching of Yoga." For instance, after the first few months of practice, you will begin to find you can read another's thoughts; they will come to you in picture form. Perhaps you will hear something happening at a long distance, when you concentrate your mind with a wish to hear. These glimpses will come, by little bits at first, but enough to give you faith, and strength, and hope. For instance, if you concentrate your thoughts on the tip of your nose, in a few days you will begin to smell most beautiful fragrance, which will be enough to show you that there are certain mental perceptions that can be made obvious without the contact of physical objects. But we must always remember that these are only the means; the aim, the end, the goal, of all this training is liberation of the soul. Absolute control of nature, and nothing short of it, must be the goal. We must be the masters, and not the slaves of nature; neither body nor mind must be our master, nor must we forget that the body is mine, and not I the body's.

A god and a demon went to learn about the Self from a great sage. They studied with him for a long time. At last the sage told them, "You yourselves are the Being you are seeking." Both of them thought that their bodies were the Self. They went back to their people quite satisfied and said, "We have learned everything that was to be learned; eat, drink, and be merry; we are the Self; there is nothing beyond us." The nature of the demon was ignorant, clouded; so he never inquired any further, but was perfectly contented with the idea that he was God, that by the Self was meant the body. The god had a purer nature. He at first committed the mistake of thinking: I, this body, am Brahman: so keep it strong and in health, and well dressed, and give it all sorts of enjoyments. But, in a few days, he found out that that could not be the meaning of the sage, their master; there must be something higher. So he came back and said, "Sir, did you teach me that this body was the Self? If so, I see all bodies die; the Self cannot die." The sage said, "Find it out; thou art That." Then the god thought that the vital forces which work the body were what the sage meant. But after a time, he found that if he ate, these vital forces remained strong, but, if he starved, they became weak. The god then went back to the sage and said, "Sir, do you mean that the vital forces are the Self?" The sage said, "Find out for yourself; thou art That." The god returned home once more, thinking that it was the mind, perhaps, that was the Self. But in a short while he saw that thoughts were so various, now good, again bad; the mind was too changeable to be the Self. He went back to the sage and said, "Sir, I do not think that the mind is the Self; did you mean that?" "No," replied the sage, "thou art That; find out for yourself." The god went home, and at last found that he was the Self, beyond all thought, one without birth or death, whom the sword cannot pierce or the fire burn, whom the air cannot dry or the water melt, the beginningless and endless, the immovable, the intangible, the omniscient, the omnipotent Being; that It was neither the body nor the mind, but beyond them all. So he was satisfied; but the poor demon did not get the truth, owing to his fondness for the body.

This world has a good many of these demoniac natures, but there are some gods too. If one proposes to teach any science to increase the power of sense-enjoyment, one finds multitudes ready for it. If one undertakes to show the supreme goal, one finds few to listen to him. Very few have the power to grasp the higher, fewer still the patience to attain to it. But there are a few also who know that even if the body can be made to live for a thousand years, the result in the end will be the same. When the forces that hold it together go away, the body must fall. No man was ever born who could stop his body one moment from changing. Body is the name of a series of changes. "As in a river the masses of water are changing before you every moment, and new masses are coming, yet taking similar form, so is it with this body." Yet the body must be kept strong and healthy. It is the best instrument we have.

This human body is the greatest body in the universe, and a human being the greatest being. Man is higher than all animals, than all angels; none is greater than man. Even the Devas (gods) will have to come down again and attain to salvation through a human body. Man alone attains to perfection, not even the Devas. According to the Jews and Mohammedans, God created man after creating the angels and everything else, and after creating man He asked the angels to come and salute him, and all did so except Iblis; so God cursed him and he became Satan. Behind this allegory is the great truth that this human birth is the greatest birth we can have. The lower creation, the animal, is dull, and manufactured mostly out of Tamas. Animals cannot have any high thoughts; nor can the angels, or Devas, attain to direct freedom without human birth. In human society, in the same way, too much wealth or too much poverty is a great impediment to the higher development of the soul. It is from the middle classes that the great ones of the world come. Here the forces are very equally adjusted and balanced.

Returning to our subject, we come next to Pranayama, controlling the breathing. What has that to do with concentrating the powers of the mind? Breath is like the fly-wheel of this machine, the body. In a big engine you find the fly-wheel first moving, and that motion is conveyed to finer and finer machinery until the most delicate and finest mechanism in the machine is in motion. The breath is that fly-wheel, supplying and regulating the motive power to everything in this body.

There was once a minister to a great king. He fell into disgrace. The king, as a punishment, ordered him to be shut up in the top of a very high tower. This was done, and the minister was left there to perish. He had a faithful wife, however, who came to the tower at night and called to her husband at the top to know what she could do to help him. He told her to return to the tower the following night and bring with her a long rope, some stout twine, pack thread, silken thread, a beetle, and a little honey. Wondering much, the good wife obeyed her husband, and brought him the desired articles. The husband directed her to attach the silken thread firmly to the beetle, then to smear its horns with a drop of honey, and to set it free on the wall of the tower, with its head pointing upwards. She obeyed all these instructions, and the beetle started on its long journey. Smelling the honey ahead it slowly crept onwards, in the hope of reaching the honey, until at last it reached the top of the tower, when the minister grasped the beetle, and got possession of the silken thread. He told his wife to tie the other end to the pack thread, and after he had drawn up the pack thread, he repeated the process with the stout twine, and lastly with the rope. Then the rest was easy. The minister descended from the tower by means of the rope, and made his escape. In this body of ours the breath motion is the "silken thread"; by laying hold of and learning to control it we grasp the pack thread of the nerve currents, and from these the stout twine of our thoughts, and lastly the rope of Prana, controlling which we reach freedom.

We do not know anything about our own bodies; we cannot know. At best we can take a dead body, and cut it in pieces, and there are some who can take a live animal and cut it in pieces in order to see what is inside the body. Still, that has nothing to do with our own bodies. We know very little about them. Why do we not? Because our attention is not discriminating enough to catch the very fine movements that are going on within. We can know of them only when the mind becomes more subtle and enters, as it were, deeper into the body. To get the subtle perception we have to begin with the grosser perceptions. We have to get hold of that which is setting the whole engine in motion. That is the Prana, the most obvious manifestation of which is the breath. Then, along with the breath, we shall slowly enter the body, which will enable us to find out about the subtle forces, the nerve currents that are moving all over the body. As soon as we perceive and learn to feel them, we shall begin to get control over them, and over the body. The mind is also set in motion: by these different nerve currents, so at last we shall reach the state of perfect control over the body and the mind, making both our servants. Knowledge is power. We have to get this power. So we must begin at the beginning, with Pranayama, restraining the Prana. This Pranayama is a long subject, and will take several lessons to illustrate it thoroughly. We shall take it part by part.

We shall gradually see the reasons for each exercise and what forces in the body are set in motion. All these things will come to us, but it requires constant practice, and the proof will come by practice. No amount of reasoning which I can give you will be proof to you, until you have demonstrated it for yourselves. As soon as you begin to feel these currents in motion all over you, doubts will vanish, but it requires hard practice every day. You must practice at least twice every day, and the best times are towards the morning and the evening. When night passes into day, and day into night, a state of relative calmness ensues. The early morning and the early evening are the two periods of calmness. Your body will have a like tendency to become calm at those times. We should take advantage of that natural condition and begin then to practice. Make it a rule not to eat until you have practiced; if you do this, the sheer force of hunger will break your laziness. In India they teach children never to eat until they have practiced or worshipped, and it becomes natural to them after a time; a boy will not feel hungry until he has bathed and practiced.

Those of you who can afford it will do better to have a room for this practice alone. Do not sleep in that room, it must be kept holy. You must not enter the room until you have bathed, and are perfectly clean in body and mind. Place flowers in that room always; they are the best surroundings for a Yogi; also pictures that are pleasing. Burn incense morning and evening. Have no quarrelling, nor anger, nor unholy thought in that room. Only allow those persons to enter it who are of the same thought as you. Then gradually there will be an atmosphere of holiness in the room, so that when you are miserable, sorrowful, doubtful, or your mind is disturbed, the very fact of entering that room will make you calm. This was the idea of the temple and the church, and in some temples and churches you will find it even now, but in the majority of them the very idea has been lost. The idea is that by keeping holy vibrations there the place becomes and remains illumined. Those who cannot afford to have a room set apart can practice anywhere they like. Sit in a straight posture, and the first thing to do is to send a current of holy thought to all creation. Mentally repeat, "Let all beings be happy; let all beings be peaceful; let all beings be blissful." So do to the east, south, north and west. The more you do that the better you will feel yourself. You will find at last that the easiest way to make ourselves healthy is to see that others are healthy, and the easiest way to make ourselves happy is to see that others are happy. After doing that, those who believe in God should pray — not for money, not for health, nor for heaven; pray for knowledge and light; every other prayer is selfish. Then the next thing to do is to think of your own body, and see that it is strong and healthy; it is the best instrument you have. Think of it as being as strong as adamant, and that with the help of this body you will cross the ocean of life. Freedom is never to be reached by the weak. Throw away all weakness. Tell your body that it is strong, tell your mind that it is strong, and have unbounded faith and hope in yourself.

CHAPTER III

Prana

Prânâyâma is not, as many think, something about breath; breath indeed has very little to do with it, if anything. Breathing is only one of the many exercises through which we get to the real Pranayama. Pranayama means the control of Prâna. According to the philosophers of India, the whole universe is composed of two materials, one of which they call Âkâsha. It is the omnipresent, all-penetrating existence. Everything that has form, everything that is the result of combination, is evolved out of this Akasha. It is the Akasha that becomes the air, that becomes the liquids, that becomes the solids; it is the Akasha that becomes the sun, the earth, the moon, the stars, the comets; it is the Akasha that becomes the human body, the animal body, the plants, every form that we see, everything that can be sensed, everything that exists. It cannot be perceived; it is so subtle that it is beyond all ordinary perception; it can only be seen when it has become gross, has taken form. At the beginning of creation there is only this Akasha. At the end of the cycle the solids, the liquids, and the gases all melt into the Akasha again, and the next creation similarly proceeds out of this Akasha.

By what power is this Akasha manufactured into this universe? By the power of Prana. Just as Akasha is the infinite, omnipresent material of this universe, so is this Prana the infinite, omnipresent manifesting power of this universe. At the beginning and at the end of a cycle everything becomes Akasha, and all the forces that are in the universe resolve back into the Prana; in the next cycle, out of this Prana is evolved everything that we call energy, everything that we call force. It is the Prana that is manifesting as motion; it is the Prana that is manifesting as gravitation, as magnetism. It is the Prana that is manifesting as the actions of the body, as the nerve currents, as thought force. From thought down to the lowest force, everything is but the manifestation of Prana. The sum total of all forces in the universe, mental or physical, when resolved back to their original state, is called Prana. "When there was neither aught nor naught, when darkness was covering darkness, what existed then? That Akasha existed without motion." The physical motion of the Prana was stopped, but it existed all the same.

At the end of a cycle the energies now displayed in the universe quiet down and become potential. At the beginning of the next cycle they start up, strike upon the Akasha, and out of the Akasha evolve these various forms, and as the Akasha changes, this Prana changes also into all these manifestations of energy. The knowledge and control of this Prana is really what is meant by Pranayama.

This opens to us the door to almost unlimited power. Suppose, for instance, a man understood the Prana perfectly, and could control it, what power on earth would not be his? He would be able to move the sun and stars out of their places, to control everything in the universe, from the atoms to the biggest suns, because he would control the Prana. This is the end and aim of Pranayama. When the Yogi becomes perfect, there will be nothing in nature not under his control. If he orders the gods or the souls of the departed to come, they will come at his bidding. All the forces of nature will obey him as slaves. When the ignorant see these powers of the Yogi, they call them the miracles. One peculiarity of the Hindu mind is that it always inquires for the last possible generalisation, leaving the details to be worked out afterwards. The question is raised in the Vedas, "What is that, knowing which, we shall know everything?" Thus, all books, and all philosophies that have been written, have been only to prove that by knowing which everything is known. If a man wants to know this universe bit by bit he must know every individual grain of sand, which means infinite time; he cannot know all of them.

Then how can knowledge be? How is it possible for a man to be all-knowing through particulars? The Yogis say that behind this particular manifestation there is a generalisation. Behind all particular ideas stands a generalised, an abstract principle; grasp it, and you have grasped everything. Just as this whole universe has been generalised in the Vedas into that One Absolute Existence, and he who has grasped that Existence has grasped the whole universe, so all forces have been generalised into this Prana, and he who has grasped the Prana has grasped all the forces of the universe, mental or physical. He who has controlled the Prana has controlled his own mind, and all the minds that exist. He who has controlled the Prana has controlled his body, and all the bodies that exist, because the Prana is the generalised manifestation of force.

How to control the Prana is the one idea of Pranayama. All the trainings and exercises in this regard are for that one end. Each man must begin where he stands, must learn how to control the things that are nearest to him. This body is very near to us, nearer than anything in the external universe, and this mind is the nearest of all. The Prana which is working this mind and body is the nearest to us of all the Prana in this universe. This little wave of the Prana which represents our own energies, mental and physical, is the nearest to us of all the waves of the infinite ocean of Prana. If we can succeed in controlling that little wave, then alone we can hope to control the whole of Prana. The Yogi who has done this gains perfection; no longer is he under any power. He becomes almost almighty, almost all-knowing. We see sects in every country who have attempted this control of Prana. In this country there are Mind-healers, Faith-healers, Spiritualists, Christian Scientists, Hypnotists, etc., and if we examine these different bodies, we shall find at the back of each this control of the Prana, whether they know it or not. If you boil all their theories down, the residuum will be that. It is the one and the same force they are manipulating, only unknowingly. They have stumbled on the discovery of a force and are using it unconsciously without knowing its nature, but it is the same as the Yogi uses, and which comes from Prana.

The Prana is the vital force in every being. Thought is the finest and highest action of Prana. Thought, again, as we see, is not all. There is also what we call instinct or unconscious thought, the lowest plane of action. If a mosquito stings us, our hand will strike it automatically, instinctively. This is one expression of thought. All reflex actions of the body belong to this plane of thought. There is again the other plane of thought, the conscious. I reason, I judge, I think, I see the pros and cons of certain things, yet that is not all. We know that reason is limited. Reason can go only to a certain extent, beyond that it cannot reach. The circle within which it runs is very very limited indeed. Yet at the same time, we find facts rush into this circle. Like the coming of comets certain things come into this circle; it is certain they come from outside the limit, although our reason cannot go beyond. The causes of the phenomena intruding themselves in this small limit are outside of this limit. The mind can exist on a still higher plane, the superconscious. When the mind has attained to that state, which is called Samâdhi — perfect concentration, superconsciousness — it goes beyond the limits of reason, and comes face to face with facts which no instinct or reason can ever know. All manipulations of the subtle forces of the body, the different manifestations of Prana, if trained, give a push to the mind, help it to go up higher, and become superconscious, from where it acts.

In this universe there is one continuous substance on every plane of existence. Physically this universe is one: there is no difference between the sun and you. The scientist will tell you it is only a fiction to say the contrary. There is no real difference between the table and me; the table is one point in the mass of matter, and I another point. Each form represents, as it were, one whirlpool in the infinite ocean of matter, of which not one is constant. Just as in a rushing stream there may be millions of whirlpools, the water in each of which is different every moment, turning round and round for a few seconds, and then passing out, replaced by a fresh quantity, so the whole universe is one constantly changing mass of matter, in which all forms of existence are so many whirlpools. A mass of matter enters into one whirlpool, say a human body, stays there for a period, becomes changed, and goes out into another, say an animal body this time, from which again after a few years, it enters into another whirlpool, called a lump of mineral. It is a constant change. Not one body is constant. There is no such thing as my body, or your body, except in words. Of the one huge mass of matter, one point is called a moon, another a sun, another a man, another the earth, another a plant, another a mineral. Not one is constant, but everything is changing, matter eternally concreting and disintegrating. So it is with the mind. Matter is represented by the ether; when the action of Prana is most subtle, this very ether, in the finer state of vibration, will represent the mind and there it will be still one unbroken mass. If you can simply get to that subtle vibration, you will see and feel that the whole universe is composed of subtle vibrations. Sometimes certain drugs have the power to take us, while as yet in the senses, to that condition. Many of you may remember the celebrated experiment of Sir Humphrey Davy, when the laughing gas overpowered him — how, during the lecture, he remained motionless, stupefied and after that, he said that the whole universe was made up of ideas. For, the time being, as it were, the gross vibrations had ceased, and only the subtle vibrations which he called ideas, were present to him. He could only see the subtle vibrations round him; everything had become thought; the whole universe was an ocean of thought, he and everyone else had become little thought whirlpools.

Thus, even in the universe of thought we find unity, and at last, when we get to the Self, we know that that Self can only be One. Beyond the vibrations of matter in its gross and subtle aspects, beyond motion there is but One. Even in manifested motion there is only unity. These facts can no more be denied. Modern physics also has demonstrated that the sum total of the energies in the universe is the same throughout. It has also been proved that this sum total of energy exists in two forms. It becomes potential, toned down, and calmed, and next it comes out manifested as all these various forces; again it goes back to the quiet state, and again it manifests. Thus it goes on evolving and involving through eternity. The control of this Prana, as before stated, is what is called Pranayama.

The most obvious manifestation of this Prana in the human body is the motion of the lungs. If that stops, as a rule all the other manifestations of force in the body will immediately stop. But there are persons who can train themselves in such a manner that the body will live on, even when this motion has stopped. There are some persons who can bury themselves for days, and yet live without breathing. To reach the subtle we must take the help of the grosser, and so, slowly travel towards the most subtle until we gain our point. Pranayama really means controlling this motion of the lungs and this motion is associated with the breath. Not that breath is producing it; on the contrary it is producing breath. This motion draws in the air by pump action. The Prana is moving the lungs, the movement of the lungs draws in the air. So Pranayama is not breathing, but controlling that muscular power which moves the lungs. That muscular power which goes out through the nerves to the muscles and from them to the lungs, making them move in a certain manner, is the Prana, which we have to control in the practice of Pranayama. When the Prana has become controlled, then we shall immediately find that all the other actions of the Prana in the body will slowly come under control. I myself have seen men who have controlled almost every muscle of the body; and why not? If I have control over certain muscles, why not over every muscle and nerve of the body? What impossibility is there? At present the control is lost, and the motion has become automatic. We cannot move our ears at will, but we know that animals can. We have not that power because we do not exercise it. This is what is called atavism.

Again, we know that motion which has become latent can be brought back to manifestation. By hard work and practice certain motions of the body which are most dormant can be brought back under perfect control. Reasoning thus we find there is no impossibility, but, on the other hand. every probability that each part of the body can be brought under perfect control. This the Yogi does through Pranayama. Perhaps some of you have read that in Pranayama, when drawing in the breath, you must fill your whole body with Prana. In the English translations Prana is given as breath, and you are inclined to ask how that is to be done. The fault is with the translator. Every part of the body can be filled with Prana, this vital force, and when you are able to do that, you can control the whole body. All the sickness and misery felt in the body will be perfectly controlled; not only so, you will be able to control another's body. Everything is infectious in this world, good or bad. If your body be in a certain state of tension, it will have a tendency to produce the same tension in others. If you are strong and healthy, those that live near you will also have the tendency to become strong and healthy, but if you are sick and weak, those around you will have the tendency to become the same. In the case of one man trying to heal another, the first idea is simply transferring his own health to the other. This is the primitive sort of healing. Consciously or unconsciously, health can be transmitted. A very strong man, living with a weak man, will make him a little stronger, whether he knows it or not. When consciously done, it becomes quicker and better in its action. Next come those cases in which a man may not be very healthy himself, yet we know that he can bring health to another. The first man, in such a case, has a little more control over the Prana, and can rouse, for the time being, his Prana, as it were, to a certain state of vibration, and transmit it to another person.

There have been cases where this process has been carried on at a distance, but in reality there is no distance in the sense of a break. Where is the distance that has a break? Is there any break between you and the sun? It is a continuous mass of matter, the sun being one part, and you another. Is there a break between one part of a river and another? Then why cannot any force travel? There is no reason against it. Cases of healing from a distance are perfectly true. The Prana can be transmitted to a very great distance; but to one genuine case, there are hundreds of frauds. This process of healing is not so easy as it is thought to be. In the most ordinary cases of such healing you will find that the healers simply take advantage of the naturally healthy state of the human body. An allopath comes and treats cholera patients, and gives them his medicines. The homoeopath comes and gives his medicines, and cures perhaps more than the allopath does, because the homoeopath does not disturb his patients, but allows nature to deal with them. The Faith-healer cures more still, because he brings the strength of his mind to bear, and rouses, through faith, the dormant Prana of the patient.

There is a mistake constantly made by Faith-healers: they think that faith directly heals a man. But faith alone does not cover all the ground. There are diseases where the worst symptoms are that the patient never thinks that he has that disease. That tremendous faith of the patient is itself one symptom of the disease, and usually indicates that he will die quickly. In such cases the principle that faith cures does not apply. If it were faith alone that cured, these patients also would be cured. It is by the Prana that real curing comes. The pure man, who has controlled the Prana, has the power of bringing it into a certain state of vibration, which can be conveyed to others, arousing in them a similar vibration. You see that in everyday actions. I am talking to you. What am I trying to do? I am, so to say, bringing my mind to a certain state of vibration, and the more I succeed in bringing it to that state, the more you will be affected by what I say. All of you know that the day I am more enthusiastic, the more you enjoy the lecture; and when I am less enthusiastic, you feel lack of interest.

The gigantic will-powers of the world, the world-movers, can bring their Prana into a high state of vibration, and it is so great and powerful that it catches others in a moment, and thousands are drawn towards them, and half the world think as they do. Great prophets of the world had the most wonderful control of the Prana, which gave them tremendous will-power;

they had brought their Prana to the highest state of motion, and this is what gave them power to sway the world. All manifestations of power arise from this control. Men may not know the secret, but this is the one explanation. Sometimes in your own body the supply of Prana gravitates more or less to one part; the balance is disturbed, and when the balance of Prana is disturbed, what we call disease is produced. To take away the superfluous Prana, or to supply the Prana that is wanting, will be curing the disease. That again is Pranayama — to learn when there is more or less Prana in one part of the body than there should be. The feelings will become so subtle that the mind will feel that there is less Prana in the toe or the finger than there should be, and will possess the power to supply it. These are among the various functions of Pranayama. They have to be learned slowly and gradually, and as you see, the whole scope of Raja-Yoga is really to teach the control and direction in different planes of the Prana. When a man has concentrated his energies, he masters the Prana that is in his body. When a man is meditating, he is also concentrating the Prana.

In an ocean there are huge waves, like mountains, then smaller waves, and still smaller, down to little bubbles, but back of all these is the infinite ocean. The bubble is connected with the infinite ocean at one end, and the huge wave at the other end. So, one may be a gigantic man, and another a little bubble, but each is connected with that infinite ocean of energy, which is the common birthright of every animal that exists. Wherever there is life, the storehouse of infinite energy is behind it. Starting as some fungus, some very minute, microscopic bubble, and all the time drawing from that infinite store-house of energy, a form is changed slowly and steadily until in course of time it becomes a plant, then an animal, then man, ultimately God. This is attained through millions of aeons, but what is time? An increase of speed, an increase of struggle, is able to bridge the gulf of time. That which naturally takes a long time to accomplish can be shortened by the intensity of the action, says the Yogi. A man may go on slowly drawing in this energy from the infinite mass that exists in the universe, and, perhaps, he will require a hundred thousand years to become a Deva, and then, perhaps, five hundred thousand years to become still higher, and, perhaps, five millions of years to become perfect. Given rapid growth, the time will be lessened. Why is it not possible, with sufficient effort, to reach this very perfection in six months or six years? There is no limit. Reason shows that. If an engine, with a certain amount of coal, runs two miles an hour, it will run the distance in less time with a greater supply of coal. Similarly, why shall not the soul, by intensifying its action, attain perfection in this very life? All beings will at last attain to that goal, we know. But who cares to wait all these millions of aeons? Why not reach it immediately, in this body even, in this human form? Why shall I not get that infinite knowledge, infinite power, now?

The ideal of the Yogi, the whole science of Yoga, is directed to the end of teaching men how, by intensifying the power of assimilation, to shorten the time for reaching perfection, instead of slowly advancing from point to point and waiting until the whole human race has become perfect. All the great prophets, saints, and seers of the world — what did they do? In one span of life they lived the whole life of humanity, traversed the whole length of time that it takes ordinary humanity to come to perfection. In one life they perfect themselves; they have no thought for anything else, never live a moment for any other idea, and thus the way is shortened for them. This is what is meant by concentration, intensifying the power of assimilation, thus shortening the time. Raja-Yoga is the science which teaches us how to gain the power of concentration.

What has Pranayama to do with spiritualism? Spiritualism is also a manifestation of Pranayama. If it be true that the departed spirits exist, only we cannot see them, it is quite probable that there may be hundreds and millions of them about us we can neither see, feel, nor touch. We may be continually passing and repassing through their bodies, and they do not see or feel us. It is a circle within a circle, universe within universe. We have five senses, and we represent Prana in a certain state of vibration. All beings in the same state of vibration will see one another, but if there are beings who represent Prana in a higher state of vibration, they will not be seen. We may increase the intensity of a light until we cannot see it at all, but there may be beings with eyes so powerful that they can see such light. Again, if its vibrations are very low, we do not see a light, but there are animals that may see it, as cats and owls. Our range of vision is only one plane of the vibrations of this Prana. Take this atmosphere, for instance; it is piled up layer on layer, but the layers nearer to the earth are denser than those above, and as you go higher the atmosphere becomes finer and finer. Or take the case of the ocean; as you go deeper and deeper the pressure of the water increases, and animals which live at the bottom of the sea can never come up, or they will be broken into pieces.

Think of the universe as an ocean of ether, consisting of layer after layer of varying degrees of vibration under the action of Prana; away from the centre the vibrations are less, nearer to it they become quicker and quicker; one order of vibration makes one plane. Then suppose these ranges of vibrations are cut into planes, so many millions of miles one set of vibration, and then so many millions of miles another still higher set of vibration, and so on. It is, therefore, probable, that those who live on the plane of a certain state of vibration will have the power of recognising one another, but will not recognise those above them. Yet, just as by the telescope and the microscope we can increase the scope of our vision, similarly we can by Yoga bring ourselves to the state of vibration of another plane, and thus enable ourselves to see what is going on there. Suppose this room is full of beings whom we do not see. They represent Prana in a certain state of vibration while we represent another. Suppose they represent a quick one, and we the opposite. Prana is the material of which they are composed, as well as we. All are parts of the same ocean of Prana, they differ only in their rate of vibration. If I can bring myself to the quick vibration, this plane will immediately change for me: I shall not see you any more; you vanish and they appear. Some of you, perhaps, know this to be true. All this bringing of the mind into a higher state of vibration is included in one word in Yoga — Samadhi. All these states of higher vibration, superconscious vibrations of the mind, are grouped in that one word, Samadhi, and the lower states of Samadhi give us visions of these beings. The highest grade of Samadhi is when we see the real thing, when we see the material out of which the whole of these grades of beings are composed, and that one lump of clay being known, we know all the clay in the universe.

Thus we see that Pranayama includes all that is true of spiritualism even. Similarly, you will find that wherever any sect or body of people is trying to search out anything occult and mystical, or hidden, what they are doing is really this Yoga, this attempt to control the Prana. You will find that wherever there is any extraordinary display of power, it is the manifestation of this Prana. Even the physical sciences can be included in Pranayama. What moves the steam engine? Prana, acting through the steam. What are all these phenomena of electricity and so forth but Prana? What is physical science? The science of Pranayama, by external means. Prana, manifesting itself as mental power, can only be controlled by mental means. That part of Pranayama which attempts to control the physical manifestations of the Prana by physical means is called physical science, and that part which tries to control the manifestations of the Prana as mental force by mental means is called Raja-Yoga.

CHAPTER IV
The Psychic Prana

According to the Yogis, there are two nerve currents in the spinal column, called Pingalâ and Idâ, and a hollow canal called Sushumnâ running through the spinal cord. At the lower end of the hollow canal is what the Yogis call the "Lotus of the Kundalini". They describe it as triangular in form in which, in the symbolical language of the Yogis, there is a power called the Kundalini, coiled up. When that Kundalini awakes, it tries to force a passage through this hollow canal, and as it rises step by step, as it were, layer after layer of the mind becomes open and all the different visions and wonderful powers come to the Yogi. When it reaches the brain, the Yogi is perfectly detached from the body and mind; the soul finds itself free. We know that the spinal cord is composed in a peculiar manner. If we take the figure eight horizontally (∞) there are two parts which are connected in the middle. Suppose you add eight after eight, piled one on top of the other, that will represent the spinal cord. The left is the Ida, the right Pingala, and that hollow canal which runs through the centre of the spinal cord is the Sushumna. Where the spinal cord ends in some of the lumbar vertebrae, a fine fibre issues downwards, and the canal runs up even within that fibre, only much finer. The canal is closed at the lower end, which is situated near what is called the sacral plexus, which, according to modern physiology, is triangular in form. The different plexuses that have their centres in the spinal canal can very well stand for the different "lotuses" of the Yogi.

The Yogi conceives of several centres, beginning with the Mulâdhâra, the basic, and ending with the Sahasrâra, the thousand-petalled Lotus in the brain. So, if we take these different plexuses as representing these lotuses, the idea of the Yogi can be understood very easily in the language of modern physiology. We know there are two sorts of actions in these nerve currents, one afferent, the other efferent; one sensory and the other motor; one centripetal, and the other centrifugal. One carries the sensations to the brain, and the other from the brain to the outer body. These vibrations are all connected with the brain in the long run. Several other facts we have to remember, in order to clear the way for the explanation which is to come. This spinal cord, at the brain, ends in a sort of bulb, in the medulla, which is not attached to the brain, but floats in a fluid in the brain, so that if there be a blow on the head the force of that blow will be dissipated in the fluid, and will not hurt the bulb. This is an important fact to remember. Secondly, we have also to know that, of all the centres, we have particularly to remember three, the Muladhara (the basic), the Sahasrara (the thousand-petalled lotus of the brain) and the Manipura (the lotus of the navel).

Next we shall take one fact from physics. We all hear of electricity and various other forces connected with it. What electricity is no one knows, but so far as it is known, it is a sort of motion. There are various other motions in the universe; what is the difference between them and electricity? Suppose this table moves — that the molecules which compose this table are moving in different directions; if they are all made to move in the same direction, it will be through electricity. Electric motion makes the molecules of a body move in the same direction. If all the air molecules in a room are made to move in the same direction, it will make a gigantic battery of electricity of the room. Another point from physiology we must remember, that the centre which regulates the respiratory system, the breathing system, has a sort of controlling action over the system of nerve currents.

Now we shall see why breathing is practised. In the first place, from rhythmical breathing comes a tendency of all the molecules in the body to move in the same direction. When mind changes into will, the nerve currents change into a motion similar to electricity, because the nerves have been proved to show polarity under the action of electric currents. This shows that when the will is transformed into the nerve currents, it is changed into something like electricity. When all the motions of the body have become perfectly rhythmical, the body has, as it were, become a gigantic battery of will. This tremendous will is exactly what the Yogi wants. This is, therefore, a physiological explanation of the breathing exercise. It tends to bring a rhythmic action in the body, and helps us, through the respiratory centre, to control the other centres. The aim of Prânâyâma here is to rouse the coiled-up power in the Muladhara, called the Kundalini.

Everything that we see, or imagine, or dream, we have to perceive in space. This is the ordinary space, called the Mahâkâsha, or elemental space. When a Yogi reads the thoughts of other men, or perceives supersensuous objects he sees them in another sort of space called the Chittâkâsha, the mental space. When perception has become objectless, and the soul shines in its own nature, it is called the Chidâkâsha, or knowledge space. When the Kundalini is aroused, and enters the canal of the Sushumna, all the perceptions are in the mental space. When it has reached that end of the canal which opens out into the brain, the objectless perception is in the knowledge space. Taking the analogy of electricity, we find that man can send a current only along a wire, (The reader should remember that this was spoken before the discovery of wireless telegraphy. — Ed.) but nature requires no wires to send her tremendous currents. This proves that the wire is not really necessary, but that only our inability to dispense with it compels us to use it.

Similarly, all the sensations and motions of the body are being sent into the brain, and sent out of it, through these wires of nerve fibres. The columns of sensory and motor fibres in the spinal cord are the Ida and Pingala of the Yogis. They are the main channels through which the afferent and efferent currents travel. But why should not the mind send news without any wire, or react without any wire? We see this is done in nature. The Yogi says, if you can do that, you have got rid of the bondage of matter. How to do it? If you can make the current pass through the Sushumna, the canal in the middle of the spinal column, you have solved the problem. The mind has made this network of the nervous system, and has to break it, so that no wires will be required to work through. Then alone will all knowledge come to us — no more bondage of body; that is why it is so important that we should get control of that Sushumna. If we can send the mental current through the hollow canal without any nerve fibres to act as wires, the Yogi says, the problem is solved, and he also says it can be done.

This Sushumna is in ordinary persons closed up at the lower extremity; no action comes through it. The Yogi proposes a practice by which it can be opened, and the nerve currents made to travel through. When a sensation is carried to a centre, the centre reacts. This reaction, in the case of automatic centres, is followed by motion; in the case of conscious centres it is followed first by perception, and secondly by motion. All perception is the reaction to action from outside. How, then, do perceptions in dreams arise? There is then no action from outside. The sensory motions, therefore, are coiled up somewhere. For instance, I see a city; the perception of that city is from the reaction to the sensations brought from outside objects comprising that city. That is to say, a certain motion in the brain molecules has been set up by the motion in the incarrying nerves, which again are set in motion by external objects in the city. Now, even after a long time I can remember the city. This memory is exactly the same phenomenon, only it is in a milder form. But whence is the action that sets up even the milder form of similar vibrations in the brain? Not certainly from the primary sensations. Therefore it must be that the sensations are coiled up somewhere, and they, by their acting, bring out the mild reaction which we call dream perception.

Now the centre where all these residual sensations are, as it were, stored up, is called the Muladhara, the root receptacle, and the coiled-up energy of action is Kundalini, "the coiled up". It is very probable that the residual motor energy is also stored up in the same centre, as, after deep study or meditation on external objects, the part of the body where the Muladhara centre is situated (probably the sacral plexus) gets heated. Now, if this coiled-up energy be roused and made active, and then consciously made to travel up the Sushumna canal, as it acts upon centre after centre, a tremendous reaction will set in. When a minute portion of energy travels along a nerve fibre and causes reaction from centres, the perception is either dream or imagination. But when by the power of long internal meditation the vast mass of energy stored up travels along the Sushumna, and strikes the centres, the reaction is tremendous, immensely superior to the reaction of dream or imagination, immensely more intense than the reaction of sense-perception. It is super-sensuous perception. And when it reaches the metropolis of all sensations, the brain, the whole brain, as it were, reacts, and the result is the full blaze of illumination, the perception of the Self. As this Kundalini force travels from centre to centre, layer after layer of the mind, as it were, opens up, and this universe is perceived by the Yogi in its fine, or causal form. Then alone the causes of this universe, both as sensation and reaction, are known as they are, and hence comes all knowledge. The causes being known, the knowledge of the effects is sure to follow.

Thus the rousing of the Kundalini is the one and only way to attaining Divine Wisdom, superconscious perception, realisation of the spirit. The rousing may come in various ways, through love for God, through the mercy of perfected sages, or through the power of the analytic will of the philosopher. Wherever there was any manifestation of what is ordinarily called supernatural power or wisdom, there a little current of Kundalini must have found its way into the Sushumna. Only, in the vast majority of such cases, people had ignorantly stumbled on some practice which set free a minute portion of the coiled-up Kundalini. All worship, consciously or unconsciously, leads to this end. The man who thinks that he is receiving response to his prayers does not know that the fulfilment comes from his own nature, that he has succeeded by the mental attitude of prayer in waking up a bit of this infinite power which is coiled up within himself. What, thus, men ignorantly worship under various names, through fear and tribulation, the Yogi declares to the world to be the real power coiled up in every being, the mother of eternal happiness, if we but know how to approach her. And Râja-Yoga is the science of religion, the rationale of all worship, all prayers, forms, ceremonies, and miracles.

CHAPTER V
The Control of Psychic Prana

We have now to deal with the exercises in Prânâyâma. We have seen that the first step, according to the Yogis, is to control the motion of the lungs. What we want to do is to feel the finer motions that are going on in the body. Our minds have become externalised, and have lost sight of the fine motions inside. If we can begin to feel them, we can begin to control them. These nerve currents go on all over the body, bringing life and vitality to every muscle, but we do not feel them. The Yogi says we can learn to do so. How? By taking up and controlling the motion of the lungs; when we have done that for a sufficient length of time, we shall be able to control the finer motions.

We now come to the exercises in Pranayama. Sit upright; the body must be kept straight. The spinal cord, although not attached to the vertebral column, is yet inside of it. If you sit crookedly you disturb this spinal cord, so let it be free. Any time that you sit crookedly and try to meditate you do yourself an injury. The three parts of the body, the chest, the neck, and the head, must be always held straight in one line. You will find that by a little practice this will come to you as easy as breathing. The second thing is to get control of the nerves. We have said that the nerve centre that controls the respiratory organs has a sort of controlling effect on the other nerves, and rhythmical breathing is, therefore, necessary. The breathing that we generally use should not be called breathing at all. It is very irregular. Then there are some natural differences of breathing between men and women.

The first lesson is just to breathe in a measured way, in and out. That will harmonise the system. When you have practiced this for some time, you will do well to join to it the repetition of some word as "Om," or any other sacred word. In India we use certain symbolical words instead of counting one, two, three, four. That is why I advise you to join the mental repetition of the "Om," or some other sacred word to the Pranayama. Let the word flow in and out with the breath, rhythmically, harmoniously, and you will find the whole body is becoming rhythmical. Then you will learn what rest is. Compared with it, sleep is not rest. Once this rest comes the most tired nerves will be calmed down, and you will find that you have never before really rested.

The first effect of this practice is perceived in the change of expression of one's face; harsh lines disappear; with calm thought calmness comes over the face. Next comes beautiful voice. I never saw a Yogi with a croaking voice. These signs come after a few months' practice. After practicing the above mentioned breathing for a few days, you should take up a higher one. Slowly fill the lungs with breath through the Idâ, the left nostril, and at the same time concentrate the mind on the nerve current. You are, as it were, sending the nerve current down the spinal column, and striking violently on the last plexus, the basic lotus which is triangular in form, the seat of the Kundalini. Then hold the current there for some time. Imagine that you are slowly drawing that nerve current with the breath through the other side, the Pingalâ, then slowly throw it out through the right nostril. This you will find a little difficult to practice. The easiest way is to stop the right nostril with the thumb, and then slowly draw in the breath through the left; then close both nostrils with thumb and forefinger, and imagine that you are sending that current down, and striking the base of the Sushumnâ; then take the thumb off, and let the breath out through the right nostril. Next inhale slowly through that nostril, keeping the other closed by the forefinger, then close both, as before. The way the Hindus practice this would be very difficult for this country, because they do it from their childhood, and their lungs are prepared for it. Here it is well to begin with four seconds, and slowly increase. Draw in four seconds, hold in sixteen seconds, then throw out in eight seconds. This makes one Pranayama. At the same time think of the basic lotus, triangular in form; concentrate the mind on that centre. The imagination can help you a great deal. The next breathing is slowly drawing the breath in, and then immediately throwing it out slowly, and then stopping the breath out, using the same numbers. The only difference is that in the first case the breath was held in, and in the second, held out. This last is the easier one. The breathing in which you hold the breath in the lungs must not be practiced too much. Do it only four times in the morning, and four times in the evening. Then you can slowly increase the time and number. You will find that you have the power to do so, and that you take pleasure in it. So very carefully and cautiously increase as you feel that you have the power, to six instead of four. It may injure you if you practice it irregularly.

Of the three processes for the purification of the nerves, described above, the first and the last are neither difficult nor dangerous. The more you practice the first one the calmer you will be. Just think of "Om," and you can practice even while you are sitting at your work. You will be all the better for it. Some day, if you practice hard, the Kundalini will be aroused. For those who practice once or twice a day, just a little calmness of the body and mind will come, and beautiful voice; only for those who can go on further with it will Kundalini be aroused, and the whole of nature will begin to change, and the book of knowledge will open. No more will you need to go to books for knowledge; your own mind will have become your book, containing infinite knowledge. I have already spoken of the Ida and Pingala currents, flowing through either side of the spinal column, and also of the Sushumna, the passage through the centre of the spinal cord. These three are present in every animal; whatever being has a spinal column has these three lines of action. But the Yogis claim that in an ordinary man the Sushumna is closed; its action is not evident while that of the other two is carrying power to different parts of the body.

The Yogi alone has the Sushumna open. When this Sushumna current opens, and begins to rise, we get beyond the sense, our minds become supersensuous, superconscious — we get beyond even the intellect, where reasoning cannot reach. To open that Sushumna is the prime object of the Yogi. According to him, along this Sushumna are ranged these centres, or, in more figurative language, these lotuses, as they are called. The lowest one is at the lower end of the spinal cord, and is called Mulâdhâra, the next higher is called Svâdhishthâna, the third Manipura, the fourth Anâhata, the fifth Vishuddha, the sixth Âjnâ and the last, which is in the brain, is the Sahasrâra, or "the thousand-petalled". Of these we have to take cognition just now of two centres only, the lowest, the Muladhara, and the highest, the Sahasrara. All energy has to be taken up from its seat in the Muladhara and brought to the Sahasrara. The Yogis claim that of all the energies that are in the human body the highest is what they call "Ojas". Now this Ojas is stored up in the brain, and the more Ojas is in a man's head, the more powerful he is, the more intellectual, the more spiritually strong. One man may speak beautiful language and beautiful thoughts, but they, do not impress people; another man speaks neither beautiful language nor beautiful thoughts, yet his words charm. Every movement of his is powerful. That is the power of Ojas.

Now in every man there is more or less of this Ojas stored up. All the forces that are working in the body in their highest become Ojas. You must remember that it is only a question of transformation. The same force which is working outside as electricity or magnetism will become changed into inner force; the same forces that are working as muscular energy will be changed into Ojas. The Yogis say that that part of the human energy which is expressed as sex energy, in sexual thought, when checked and controlled, easily becomes changed into Ojas, and as the Muladhara guides these, the Yogi pays particular attention to that centre. He tries to take up all his sexual energy and convert it into Ojas. It is only the chaste man or woman who can make the Ojas rise and store it in the brain; that is why chastity has always been considered the highest virtue. A man feels that if he is unchaste, spirituality goes away, he loses mental vigour and moral stamina. That is why in all the religious orders in the world which have produced spiritual giants you will always find absolute chastity insisted upon. That is why the monks came into existence, giving up marriage. There must be perfect chastity in thought, word, and deed; without it the practice of Raja-Yoga is dangerous, and may lead to insanity. If people practice Raja-Yoga and at the same time lead an impure life, how can they expect to become Yogis?

CHAPTER VI
Pratyahara and Dharana

The next step is called Pratyâhâra. What is this? You know how perceptions come. First of all there are the external instruments, then the internal organs acting in the body through the brain centres, and there is the mind. When these come together and attach themselves to some external object, then we perceive it. At the same time it is a very difficult thing to concentrate the mind and attach it to one organ only; the mind is a slave.

We hear "Be good," and "Be good," and "Be good," taught all over the world. There is hardly a child, born in any country in the world, who has not been told, "Do not steal," "Do not tell a lie," but nobody tells the child how he can help doing them. Talking will not help him. Why should he not become a thief? We do not teach him how not to steal; we simply tell him, "Do not steal." Only when we teach him to control his mind do we really help him. All actions, internal and external, occur when the mind joins itself to certain centres, called the organs. Willingly or unwillingly it is drawn to join itself to the centres, and that is why people do foolish deeds and feel miserable, which, if the mind were under control, they would not do. What would be the result of controlling the mind? It then would not join itself to the centres of perception, and, naturally, feeling and willing would be under control. It is clear so far. Is it possible? It is perfectly possible. You see it in modern times; the faith-healers teach people to deny misery and pain and evil. Their philosophy is rather roundabout, but it is a part of Yoga upon which they have somehow stumbled. Where they succeed in making a person throw off suffering by denying it, they really use a part of Pratyahara, as they make the mind of the person strong enough to ignore the senses. The hypnotists in a similar manner, by their suggestion, excite in the patient a sort of morbid Pratyahara for the time being. The so-called hypnotic suggestion can only act upon a weak mind. And until the operator, by means of fixed gaze or otherwise, has succeeded in putting the mind of the subject in a sort of passive, morbid condition, his suggestions never work.

Now the control of the centres which is established in a hypnotic patient or the patient of faith-healing, by the operator, for a time, is reprehensible, because it leads to ultimate ruin. It is not really controlling the brain centres by the power of one's own will, but is, as it were, stunning the patient's mind for a time by sudden blows which another's will delivers to it. It is not checking by means of reins and muscular strength the mad career of a fiery team, but rather by asking another to deliver heavy blows on the heads of the horses, to stun them for a time into gentleness. At each one of these processes the man operated upon loses a part of his mental energies, till at last, the mind, instead of gaining the power of perfect control, becomes a shapeless, powerless mass, and the only goal of the patient is the lunatic asylum.

Every attempt at control which is not voluntary, not with the controller's own mind, is not only disastrous, but it defeats the end. The goal of each soul is freedom, mastery — freedom from the slavery of matter and thought, mastery of external and internal nature. Instead of leading towards that, every will-current from another, in whatever form it comes, either as direct control of organs, or as forcing to control them while under a morbid condition, only rivets one link more to the already existing heavy chain of bondage of past thoughts, past superstitions. Therefore, beware how you allow yourselves to be acted upon by others. Beware how you unknowingly bring another to ruin. True, some succeed in doing good to many for a time, by giving a new trend to their propensities, but at the same time, they bring ruin to millions by the unconscious suggestions they throw around, rousing in men and women that morbid, passive, hypnotic condition which makes them almost soulless at last. Whosoever, therefore, asks any one to believe blindly, or drags people behind him by the controlling power of his superior will, does an injury to humanity, though he may not intend it.

Therefore use your own minds, control body and mind yourselves, remember that until you are a diseased person, no extraneous will can work upon you; avoid everyone, however great and good he may be, who asks you to believe blindly. All over the world there have been dancing and jumping and howling sects, who spread like infection when they begin to sing and dance and preach; they also are a sort of hypnotists. They exercise a singular control for the time being over sensitive persons, alas! often, in the long run, to degenerate whole races. Ay, it is healthier for the individual or the race to remain wicked than be made apparently good by such morbid extraneous control. One's heart sinks to think of the amount of injury done to humanity by such irresponsible yet well-meaning religious fanatics. They little know that the minds which attain to sudden spiritual upheaval under their suggestions, with music and prayers, are simply making themselves passive, morbid, and powerless, and opening themselves to any other suggestion, be it ever so evil. Little do these ignorant, deluded persons dream that whilst they are congratulating themselves upon their miraculous power to transform human hearts, which power they think was poured upon them by some Being above the clouds, they are sowing the seeds of future decay, of crime, of lunacy, and of death. Therefore, beware of everything that takes away your freedom. Know that it is dangerous, and avoid it by all the means in your power.

He who has succeeded in attaching or detaching his mind to or from the centres at will has succeeded in Pratyahara, which means, "gathering towards," checking the outgoing powers of the mind, freeing it from the thraldom of the senses. When we can do this, we shall really possess character; then alone we shall have taken a long step towards freedom; before that we are mere machines.

How hard it is to control the mind! Well has it been compared to the maddened monkey. There was a monkey, restless by his own nature, as all monkeys are. As if that were not enough some one made him drink freely of wine, so that he became still more restless. Then a scorpion stung him. When a man is stung by a scorpion, he jumps about for a whole day; so the poor monkey found his condition worse than ever. To complete his misery a demon entered into him. What language can describe the uncontrollable restlessness of that monkey? The human mind is like that monkey, incessantly active by its own nature; then it becomes drunk with the wine of desire, thus increasing its turbulence. After desire takes possession comes the sting of the scorpion of jealousy at the success of others, and last of all the demon of pride enters the mind, making it think itself of all importance. How hard to control such a mind!

The first lesson, then, is to sit for some time and let the mind run on. The mind is bubbling up all the time. It is like that monkey jumping about. Let the monkey jump as much as he can; you simply wait and watch. Knowledge is power, says the proverb, and that is true. Until you know what the mind is doing you cannot control it. Give it the rein; many hideous thoughts may come into it; you will be astonished that it was possible for you to think such thoughts. But you will find that each day the mind's vagaries are becoming less and less violent, that each day it is becoming calmer. In the first few months you will find that the mind will have a great many thoughts, later you will find that they have somewhat decreased, and in a few more months they will be fewer and fewer, until at last the mind will be under perfect control; but we must patiently practice every day. As soon as the steam is turned on, the engine must run; as soon as things are before us we must perceive; so a man, to prove that he is not a machine, must demonstrate that he is under the control of nothing. This controlling of the mind, and not allowing it to join itself to the centres, is Pratyahara. How is this practised? It is a tremendous work, not to be done in a day. Only after a patient, continuous struggle for years can we succeed.

After you have practised Pratyahara for a time, take the next step, the Dhâr anâ, holding the mind to certain points. What is meant by holding the mind to certain points? Forcing the mind to feel certain parts of the body to the exclusion of others. For instance, try to feel only the hand, to the exclusion of other parts of the body. When the Chitta, or mind-stuff, is confined and limited to a certain place it is Dharana. This Dharana is of various sorts, and along with it, it is better to have a little play of the imagination. For instance, the mind should be made to think of one point in the heart. That is very difficult; an easier way is to imagine a lotus there. That lotus is full of light, effulgent light. Put the mind there. Or think of the lotus in the brain as full of light, or of the different centres in the Sushumna mentioned before.

The Yogi must always practice. He should try to live alone; the companionship of different sorts of people distracts the mind; he should not speak much, because to speak distracts the mind; not work much, because too much work distracts the mind; the mind cannot be controlled after a whole day's hard work. One observing the above rules becomes a Yogi. Such is the power of Yoga that even the least of it will bring a great amount of benefit. It will not hurt anyone, but will benefit everyone. First of all, it will tone down nervous excitement, bring calmness, enable us to see things more clearly. The temperament will be better, and the health will be better. Sound health will be one of the first signs, and a beautiful voice. Defects in the voice will be changed. This will be among the first of the many effects that will come. Those who practise hard will get many other signs. Sometimes there will be sounds, as a peal of bells heard at a distance, commingling, and falling on the ear as one continuous sound. Sometimes things will be seen, little specks of light floating and becoming bigger and bigger; and when these things come, know that you are progressing fast.

Those who want to be Yogis, and practice hard, must take care of their diet at first. But for those who want only a little practice for everyday business sort of life, let them not eat too much; otherwise they may eat whatever they please. For those who want to make rapid progress, and to practice hard, a strict diet is absolutely necessary. They will find it advantageous to live only on milk and cereals for some months. As the organisation becomes finer and finer, it will be found in the beginning that the least irregularity throws one out of balance. One bit of food more or less will disturb the whole system, until one gets perfect control, and then one will be able to eat whatever one likes.

When one begins to concentrate, the dropping of a pin will seem like a thunderbolt going through the brain. As the organs get finer, the perceptions get finer. These are the stages through which we have to pass, and all those who persevere will succeed. Give up all argumentation and other distractions. Is there anything in dry intellectual jargon? It only throws the mind off its balance and disturbs it. Things of subtler planes have to be realised. Will talking do that? So give up all vain talk. Read only those books which have been written by persons who have had realisation.

Be like the pearl oyster. There is a pretty Indian fable to the effect that if it rains when the star Svâti is in the ascendant, and a drop of rain falls into an oyster, that drop becomes a pearl. The oysters know this, so they come to the surface when that star shines, and wait to catch the precious raindrop. When a drop falls into them, quickly the oysters close their shells and dive down to the bottom of the sea, there to patiently develop the drop into the pearl. We should be like that. First hear, then understand, and then, leaving all distractions, shut your minds to outside influences, and devote yourselves to developing the truth within you. There is the danger of frittering away your energies by taking up an idea only for its novelty, and then giving it up for another that is newer. Take one thing up and do it, and see the end of it, and before you have seen the end, do not give it up. He who can become mad with an idea, he alone sees light. Those that only take a nibble here and a nibble there will never attain anything. They may titillate their nerves for a moment, but there it will end. They will be slaves in the hands of nature, and will never get beyond the senses.

Those who really want to be Yogis must give up, once for all, this nibbling at things. Take up one idea. Make that one idea your life — think of it, dream of it, live on that idea. Let the brain, muscles, nerves, every part of your body, be full of that idea, and just leave every other idea alone. This is the way to success, and this is the way great spiritual giants are produced. Others are mere talking machines. If we really want to be blessed, and make others blessed, we must go deeper. The first step is not to disturb the mind, not to associate with persons whose ideas are disturbing. All of you know that certain persons, certain places, certain foods, repel you. Avoid them; and those who want to go to the highest, must avoid all company, good or bad. Practise hard; whether you live or die does not matter. You have to plunge in and work, without thinking of the result. If you are brave enough, in six months you will be a perfect Yogi. But those who take up just a bit of it and a little of everything else make no progress. It is of no use simply to take a course of lessons. To those who are full of Tamas, ignorant and dull — those whose minds never get fixed on any idea, who only crave for something to amuse them — religion and philosophy are simply objects of entertainment. These are the unpersevering. They hear a talk, think it very nice, and then go home and forget all about it. To succeed, you must have tremendous perseverance, tremendous will. "I will drink the ocean," says the persevering soul, "at my will mountains will crumble up." Have that sort of energy, that sort of will, work hard, and you will reach the goal.

CHAPTER VII
Dhyana and Samadhi

We have taken a cursory view of the different steps in Râja-Yoga, except the finer ones, the training in concentration, which is the goal to which Raja-Yoga will lead us. We see, as human beings, that all our knowledge which is called rational is referred to consciousness. My consciousness of this table, and of your presence, makes me know that the table and you are here. At the same time, there is a very great part of my existence of which I am not conscious. All the different organs inside the body, the different parts of the brain — nobody is conscious of these.

When I eat food, I do it consciously; when I assimilate it, I do it unconsciously. When the food is manufactured into blood, it is done unconsciously. When out of the blood all the different parts of my body are strengthened, it is done unconsciously. And yet it is I who am doing all this; there cannot be twenty people in this one body. How do I know that I do it, and nobody else? It may be urged that my business is only in eating and assimilating the food, and that strengthening the body by the food is done for me by somebody else. That cannot be, because it can be demonstrated that almost every action of which we are now unconscious can be brought up to the plane of consciousness. The heart is beating apparently without our control. None of us here can control the heart; it goes on its own way. But by practice men can bring even the heart under control, until it will just beat at will, slowly, or quickly, or almost stop. Nearly every part of the body can be brought under control. What does this show? That the functions which are beneath consciousness are also performed by us, only we are doing it unconsciously. We have, then, two planes in which the human mind works. First is the conscious plane, in which all work is always accompanied with the feeling of egoism. Next comes the unconscious plane, where all work is unaccompanied by the feeling of egoism. That part of mind-work which is unaccompanied with the feeling of egoism is unconscious work, and that part which is accompanied with the feeling of egoism is conscious work. In the lower animals this unconscious work is called instinct. In higher animals, and in the highest of all animals, man, what is called conscious work prevails.

But it does not end here. There is a still higher plane upon which the mind can work. It can go beyond consciousness. Just as unconscious work is beneath consciousness, so there is another work which is above consciousness, and which also is not accompanied with the feeling of egoism. The feeling of egoism is only on the middle plane. When the mind is above or below that line, there is no feeling of "I", and yet the mind works. When the mind goes beyond this line of self-consciousness, it is called Samâdhi or superconsciousness. How, for instance, do we know that a man in Samadhi has not gone below consciousness, has not degenerated instead of going higher? In both cases the works are unaccompanied with egoism. The answer is, by the effects, by the results of the work, we know that which is below, and that which is above. When a man goes into deep sleep, he enters a plane beneath consciousness. He works the body all the time, he breathes, he moves the body, perhaps, in his sleep, without any accompanying feeling of ego; he is unconscious, and when he returns from his sleep, he is the same man who went into it. The sum total of the knowledge which he had before he went into the sleep remains the same; it does not increase at all. No enlightenment comes. But when a man goes into Samadhi, if he goes into it a fool, he comes out a sage.

What makes the difference? From one state a man comes out the very same man that he went in, and from another state the man comes out enlightened, a sage, a prophet, a saint, his whole character changed, his life changed, illumined. These are the two effects. Now the effects being different, the causes must be different. As this illumination with which a man comes back from Samadhi is much higher than can be got from unconsciousness, or much higher than can be got by reasoning in a conscious state, it must, therefore, be superconsciousness, and Samadhi is called the superconscious state.

This, in short, is the idea of Samadhi. What is its application? The application is here. The field of reason, or of the conscious workings of the mind, is narrow and limited. There is a little circle within which human reason must move. It cannot go beyond. Every attempt to go beyond is impossible, yet it is beyond this circle of reason that there lies all that humanity holds most dear. All these questions, whether there is an immortal soul, whether there is a God, whether there is any supreme intelligence guiding this universe or not, are beyond the field of reason. Reason can never answer these questions. What does reason say? It says, "I am agnostic; I do not know either yea or nay." Yet these questions are so important to us. Without a proper answer to them, human life will be purposeless. All our ethical theories, all our moral attitudes, all that is good and great in human nature, have been moulded upon answers that have come from beyond the circle. It is very important, therefore, that we should have answers to these questions. If life is only a short play, if the universe is only a "fortuitous combination of atoms," then why should I do good to another? Why should there be mercy, justice, or fellow-feeling? The best thing for this world would be to make hay while the sun shines, each man for himself. If there is no hope, why should I love my brother, and not cut his throat? If there is nothing beyond, if there is no freedom, but only rigorous dead laws, I should only try to make myself happy here. You will find people saying nowadays that they have utilitarian grounds as the basis of morality. What is this basis? Procuring the greatest amount of happiness to the greatest number. Why should I do this? Why should I not produce the greatest unhappiness to the greatest number, if that serves my purpose? How will utilitarians answer this question? How do you know what is right, or what is wrong? I am impelled by my desire for happiness, and I fulfil it, and it is in my nature; I know nothing beyond. I have these desires, and must fulfil them; why should you complain? Whence come all these truths about human life, about morality, about the immortal soul, about God, about love and sympathy, about being good, and, above all, about being unselfish?

All ethics, all human action and all human thought, hang upon this one idea of unselfishness. The whole idea of human life can be put into that one word, unselfishness. Why should we be unselfish? Where is the necessity, the force, the power, of my being unselfish? You call yourself a rational man, a utilitarian; but if you do not show me a reason for utility, I say you are irrational. Show me the reason why I should not be selfish. To ask one to be unselfish may be good as poetry, but poetry is not reason. Show me a reason. Why shall I be unselfish, and why be good? Because Mr. and Mrs. So-and-so say so does not weigh with me. Where is the utility of my being unselfish? My utility is to be selfish if utility means the greatest amount of happiness. What is the answer? The utilitarian can never give it. The answer is that this world is only one drop in an infinite ocean, one link in an infinite chain. Where did those that preached unselfishness, and taught it to the human race, get this idea? We know it is not instinctive; the animals, which have instinct, do not know it. Neither is it reason; reason does not know anything about these ideas. Whence then did they come?

We find, in studying history, one fact held in common by all the great teachers of religion the world ever had. They all claim to have got their truths from beyond, only many of them did not know where they got them from. For instance, one would say that an angel came down in the form of a human being, with wings, and said to him, "Hear, O man, this is the message." Another says that a Deva, a bright being, appeared to him. A third says he dreamed that his ancestor came and told him certain things. He did not know anything beyond that. But this is common that all claim that this knowledge has come to them from beyond, not through their reasoning power. What does the science of Yoga teach? It teaches that they were right in claiming that all this knowledge came to them from beyond reasoning, but that it came from within themselves.

The Yogi teaches that the mind itself has a higher state of existence, beyond reason, a superconscious state, and when the mind gets to that higher state, then this knowledge, beyond reasoning, comes to man. Metaphysical and transcendental knowledge comes to that man. This state of going beyond reason, transcending ordinary human nature, may sometimes come by chance to a man who does not understand its science; he, as it were, stumbles upon it. When he stumbles upon it, he generally interprets it as coming from outside. So this explains why an inspiration, or transcendental knowledge, may be the same in different countries, but in one country it will seem to come through an angel, and in another through a Deva, and in a third through God. What does it mean? It means that the mind brought the knowledge by its own nature, and that the finding of the knowledge was interpreted according to the belief and education of the person through whom it came. The real fact is that these various men, as it were, stumbled upon this superconscious state.

The Yogi says there is a great danger in stumbling upon this state. In a good many cases there is the danger of the brain being deranged, and, as a rule, you will find that all those men, however great they were, who had stumbled upon this superconscious state without understanding it, groped in the dark, and generally had, along with their knowledge, some quaint superstition. They opened themselves to hallucinations. Mohammed claimed that the Angel Gabriel came to him in a cave one day and took him on the heavenly horse, Harak, and he visited the heavens. But with all that, Mohammed spoke some wonderful truths. If you read the Koran, you find the most wonderful truths mixed with superstitions. How will you explain it? That man was inspired, no doubt, but that inspiration was, as it were, stumbled upon. He was not a trained Yogi, and did not know the reason of what he was doing. Think of the good Mohammed did to the world, and think of the great evil that has been done through his fanaticism! Think of the millions massacred through his teachings, mothers bereft of their children, children made orphans, whole countries destroyed, millions upon millions of people killed!

So we see this danger by studying the lives of great teachers like Mohammed and others. Yet we find, at the same time, that they were all inspired. Whenever a prophet got into the superconscious state by heightening his emotional nature, he brought away from it not only some truths, but some fanaticism also, some superstition which injured the world as much as the greatness of the teaching helped. To get any reason out of the mass of incongruity we call human life, we have to transcend our reason, but we must do it scientifically, slowly, by regular practice, and we must cast off all superstition. We must take up the study of the superconscious state just as any other science. On reason we must have to lay our foundation, we must follow reason as far as it leads, and when reason fails, reason itself will show us the way to the highest plane. When you hear a man say, "I am inspired," and then talk irrationally, reject it. Why? Because these three states — instinct, reason, and superconsciousness, or the unconscious, conscious, and superconscious states — belong to one and the same mind. There are not three minds in one man, but one state of it develops into the others. Instinct develops into reason, and reason into the transcendental consciousness; therefore, not one of the states contradicts the others. Real inspiration never contradicts reason, but fulfils it. Just as you find the great prophets saying, "I come not to destroy but to fulfil," so inspiration always comes to fulfil reason, and is in harmony with it.

All the different steps in Yoga are intended to bring us scientifically to the superconscious state, or Samadhi. Furthermore, this is a most vital point to understand, that inspiration is as much in every man's nature as it was in that of the ancient prophets. These prophets were not unique; they were men as you or I. They were great Yogis. They had gained this superconsciousness, and you and I can get the same. They were not peculiar people. The very fact that one man ever reached that state, proves that it is possible for every man to do so. Not only is it possible, but every man must, eventually, get to that state, and that is religion. Experience is the only teacher we have. We may talk and reason all our lives, but we shall not understand a word of truth, until we experience it ourselves. You cannot hope to make a man a surgeon by simply giving him a few books. You cannot satisfy my curiosity to see a country by showing me a map; I must have actual experience. Maps can only create curiosity in us to get more perfect knowledge. Beyond that, they have no value whatever. Clinging to books only degenerates the human mind. Was there ever a more horrible blasphemy than the statement that all the knowledge of God is confined to this or that book? How dare men call God infinite, and yet try to compress Him within the covers of a little book! Millions of people have been killed because they did not believe what the books said, because they would not see all the knowledge of God within the covers of a book. Of course this killing and murdering has gone by, but the world is still tremendously bound up in a belief in books.

In order to reach the superconscious state in a scientific manner it is necessary to pass through the various steps of Raja-Yoga I have been teaching. After Pratyâhâra and Dhâranâ, we come to Dhyâna, meditation. When the mind has been trained to remain fixed on a certain internal or external location, there comes to it the power of flowing in an unbroken current, as it were, towards that point. This state is called Dhyana. When one has so intensified the power of Dhyana as to be able to reject the external part of perception and remain meditating only on the internal part, the meaning, that state is called Samadhi. The three — Dharana, Dhyana, and Samadhi — together, are called Samyama. That is, if the mind can first concentrate upon an object, and then is able to continue in that concentration for a length of time, and then, by continued concentration, to dwell only on the internal part of the perception of which the object was the effect, everything comes under the control of such a mind.

This meditative state is the highest state of existence. So long as there is desire, no real happiness can come. It is only the contemplative, witness-like study of objects that brings to us real enjoyment and happiness. The animal has its happiness in the senses, the man in his intellect, and the god in spiritual contemplation. It is only to the soul that has attained to this contemplative state that the world really becomes beautiful. To him who desires nothing, and does not mix himself up with them, the manifold changes of nature are one panorama of beauty and sublimity.

These ideas have to be understood in Dhyana, or meditation. We hear a sound. First, there is the external vibration; second, the nerve motion that carries it to the mind; third, the reaction from the mind, along with which flashes the knowledge of the object which was the external cause of these different changes from the ethereal vibrations to the mental reactions. These three are called in Yoga, Shabda (sound), Artha (meaning), and Jnâna (knowledge). In the language of physics and physiology they are called the ethereal vibration, the motion in the nerve and brain, and the mental reaction. Now these, though distinct processes, have become mixed up in such a fashion as to become quite indistinct. In fact, we cannot now perceive any of these, we only perceive their combined effect, what we call the external object. Every act of perception includes these three, and there is no reason why we should not be able to distinguish them.

When, by the previous preparations, it becomes strong and controlled, and has the power of finer perception, the mind should be employed in meditation. This meditation must begin with gross objects and slowly rise to finer and finer, until it becomes objectless. The mind should first be employed in perceiving the external causes of sensations, then the internal motions, and then its own reaction. When it has succeeded in perceiving the external causes of sensations by themselves, the mind will acquire the power of perceiving all fine material existences, all fine bodies and forms. When it can succeed in perceiving the motions inside by themselves, it will gain the control of all mental waves, in itself or in others, even before they have translated themselves into physical energy; and when he will be able to perceive the mental reaction by itself, the Yogi will acquire the knowledge of everything, as every sensible object, and every thought is the result of this reaction. Then will he have seen the very foundations of his mind, and it will be under his perfect control.

Different powers will come to the Yogi, and if he yields to the temptations of any one of these, the road to his further progress will be barred. Such is the evil of running after enjoyments. But if he is strong enough to reject even these miraculous powers, he will attain to the goal of Yoga, the complete suppression of the waves in the ocean of the mind. Then the glory of the soul, undisturbed by the distractions of the mind, or motions of the body, will shine in its full effulgence; and the Yogi will find himself as he is and as he always was, the essence of knowledge, the immortal, the all-pervading.

Samadhi is the property of every human being — nay, every animal. From the lowest animal to the highest angel, some time or other, each one will have to come to that state, and then, and then alone, will real religion begin for him. Until then we only struggle towards that stage. There is no difference now between us and those who have no religion, because we have no experience. What is concentration good for, save to bring us to this experience? Each one of the steps to attain Samadhi has been reasoned out, properly adjusted, scientifically organised, and, when faithfully practiced, will surely lead us to the desired end. Then will all sorrows cease, all miseries vanish; the seeds for actions will be burnt, and the soul will be free for ever.

CHAPTER VIII
Raja-Yoga in Brief

The following is a summary of Râja-Yoga freely translated from the Kurma-Purâna.

The fire of Yoga burns the cage of sin that is around a man. Knowledge becomes purified and Nirvâna is directly obtained. From Yoga comes knowledge; knowledge again helps the Yogi. He who combines in himself both Yoga and knowledge, with him the Lord is pleased. Those that practice Mahâyoga, either once a day, or twice a day, or thrice, or always, know them to be gods. Yoga is divided into two parts. One is called Abhâva, and the other, Mahayoga. Where one's self is meditated upon as zero, and bereft of quality, that is called Abhava. That in which one sees the self as full of bliss and bereft of all impurities, and one with God, is called Mahayoga. The Yogi, by each one, realises his Self. The other Yogas that we read and hear of, do not deserve to be ranked with the excellent Mahayoga in which the Yogi finds himself and the whole universe as God. This is the highest of all Yogas.

Yama, Niyama, Âsana, Prânâyâma, Pratyâhâra, Dhârâna, Dhyâna, and Samâdhi are the steps in Raja-Yoga, of which non-injury, truthfulness, non-covetousness, chastity, not receiving anything from another are called Yama. This purifies the mind, the Chitta. Never producing pain by thought, word, and deed, in any living being, is what is called Ahimsâ, non-injury. There is no virtue higher than non-injury. There is no happiness higher than what a man obtains by this attitude of non-offensiveness, to all creation. By truth we attain fruits of work. Through truth everything is attained. In truth everything is established. Relating facts as they are — this is truth. Not taking others' goods by stealth or by force, is called Asteya, non-covetousness. Chastity in thought, word, and deed, always, and in all conditions, is what is called Brahmacharya. Not receiving any present from anybody, even when one is suffering terribly, is what is called Aparigraha. The idea is, when a man receives a gift from another, his heart becomes impure, he becomes low, he loses his independence, he becomes bound and attached.

The following are helps to success in Yoga and are called Niyama or regular habits and observances; Tapas, austerity; Svâdhyâya, study; Santosha, contentment; Shaucha, purity; Ishvara-pranidhâna, worshipping God. Fasting, or in other ways controlling the body, is called physical Tapas. Repeating the Vedas and other Mantras, by which the Sattva material in the body is purified, is called study, Svadhyaya. There are three sorts of repetitions of these Mantras. One is called the verbal, another semi-verbal, and the third mental. The verbal or audible is the lowest, and the inaudible is the highest of all. The repetition which is loud is the verbal; the next one is where only the lips move, but no sound is heard. The inaudible repetition of the Mantra, accompanied with the thinking of its meaning, is called the "mental repetition," and is the highest. The sages have said that there are two sorts of purification, external and internal. The purification of the body by water, earth, or other materials is the external purification, as bathing etc. Purification of the mind by truth, and by all the other virtues, is what is called internal purification. Both are necessary. It is not sufficient that a man should be internally pure and externally dirty. When both are not attainable the internal purity is the better, but no one will be a Yogi until he has both. Worship of God is by praise, by thought, by devotion.

We have spoken about Yama and Niyama. The next is Asana (posture). The only thing to understand about it is leaving the body free, holding the chest, shoulders, and head straight. Then comes Pranayama. Prana means the vital forces in one's own body, Âyâma means controlling them. There are three sorts of Pranayama, the very simple, the middle, and the very high. Pranayama is divided into three parts: filling, restraining, and emptying. When you begin with twelve seconds it is the lowest

Pranayama; when you begin with twenty-four seconds it is the middle Pranayama; that Pranayama is the best which begins with thirty-six seconds. In the lowest kind of Pranayama there is perspiration, in the medium kind, quivering of the body, and in the highest Pranayama levitation of the body and influx of great bliss. There is a Mantra called the Gâyatri. It is a very holy verse of the Vedas. "We meditate on the glory of that Being who has produced this universe; may He enlighten our minds." Om is joined to it at the beginning and the end. In one Pranayama repeat three Gayatris. In all books they speak of Pranayama being divided into Rechaka (rejecting or exhaling), Puraka (inhaling), and Kurnbhaka (restraining, stationary). The Indriyas, the organs of the senses, are acting outwards and coming in contact with external objects. Bringing them under the control of the will is what is called Pratyahara or gathering towards oneself. Fixing the mind on the lotus of the heart, or on the centre of the head, is what is called Dharana. Limited to one spot, making that spot the base, a particular kind of mental waves rises; these are not swallowed up by other kinds of waves, but by degrees become prominent, while all the others recede and finally disappear. Next the multiplicity of these waves gives place to unity and one wave only is left in the mind. This is Dhyana, meditation. When no basis is necessary, when the whole of the mind has become one wave, one-formedness, it is called Samadhi. Bereft of all help from places and centres, only the meaning of the thought is present. If the mind can be fixed on the centre for twelve seconds it will be a Dharana, twelve such Dharanas will be a Dhyana, and twelve such Dhyanas will be a Samadhi.

Where there is fire, or in water or on ground which is strewn with dry leaves, where there are many ant-hills, where there are wild animals, or danger, where four streets meet, where there is too much noise, where there are many wicked persons, Yoga must not be practiced. This applies more particularly to India. Do not practice when the body feels very lazy or ill, or when the mind is very miserable and sorrowful. Go to a place which is well hidden, and where people do not come to disturb you. Do not choose dirty places. Rather choose beautiful scenery, or a room in your own house which is beautiful. When you practice, first salute all the ancient Yogis, and your own Guru, and God, and then begin.

Dhyana is spoken of, and a few examples are given of what to meditate upon. Sit straight, and look at the tip of your nose. Later on we shall come to know how that concentrates the mind, how by controlling the two optic nerves one advances a long way towards the control of the arc of reaction, and so to the control of the will. Here are a few specimens of meditation. Imagine a lotus upon the top of the head, several inches up, with virtue as its centre, and knowledge as its stalk. The eight petals of the lotus are the eight powers of the Yogi. Inside, the stamens and pistils are renunciation. If the Yogi refuses the external powers he will come to salvation. So the eight petals of the lotus are the eight powers, but the internal stamens and pistils are extreme renunciation, the renunciation of all these powers. Inside of that lotus think of the Golden One, the Almighty, the Intangible, He whose name is Om, the Inexpressible, surrounded with effulgent light. Meditate on that. Another meditation is given. Think of a space in your heart, and in the midst of that space think that a flame is burning. Think of that flame as your own soul and inside the flame is another effulgent light, and that is the Soul of your soul, God. Meditate upon that in the heart. Chastity, non-injury, forgiving even the greatest enemy, truth, faith in the Lord, these are all different Vrittis. Be not afraid if you are not perfect in all of these; work, they will come. He who has given up all attachment, all fear, and all anger, he whose whole soul has gone unto the Lord, he who has taken refuge in the Lord, whose heart has become purified, with whatsoever desire he comes to the Lord, He will grant that to him. Therefore worship Him through knowledge, love, or renunciation.

"He who hates none, who is the friend of all, who is merciful to all, who has nothing of his own, who is free from egoism, who is even-minded in pain and pleasure, who is forbearing, who is always satisfied, who works always in Yoga, whose self has become controlled, whose will is firm, whose mind and intellect are given up unto Me, such a one is My beloved Bhakta. From whom comes no disturbance, who cannot be disturbed by others, who is free from joy, anger, fear, and anxiety, such a one is My beloved. He who does not depend on anything, who is pure and active, who does not care whether good comes or evil, and never becomes miserable, who has given up all efforts for himself; who is the same in praise or in blame, with a silent, thoughtful mind, blessed with what little comes in his way, homeless, for the whole world is his home, and who is steady in his ideas, such a one is My beloved Bhakta." Such alone become Yogis.

*   *   *   *

There was a great god-sage called Nârada. Just as there are sages among mankind, great Yogis, so there are great Yogis among the gods. Narada was a good Yogi, and very great. He travelled everywhere. One day he was passing through a forest, and saw a man who had been meditating until the white ants had built a huge mound round his body — so long had he been sitting in that position. He said to Narada, "Where are you going?" Narada replied, "I am going to heaven." "Then ask God when He will be merciful to me; when I shall attain freedom." Further on Narada saw another man. He was jumping about, singing, dancing, and said, "Oh, Narada, where are you going?" His voice and his gestures were wild. Narada said, "I am going to heaven." "Then, ask when I shall be free." Narada went on. In the course of time he came again by the same road, and there was the man who had been meditating with the ant-hill round him. He said, "Oh, Narada, did you ask the Lord about me?" "Oh, yes." "What did He say?" "The Lord told me that you would attain freedom in four more births." Then the man began to weep and wail, and said, "I have meditated until an ant-hill has grown around me, and I have four more births yet!" Narada went to the other man. "Did you ask my question?" "Oh, yes. Do you see this tamarind tree? I have to tell you that as many leaves as there are on that tree, so many times, you shall be born, and then you shall attain freedom." The man began to dance for joy, and said, "I shall have freedom after such a short time!" A voice came, "My child, you will have freedom this minute." That was the reward for his perseverance. He was ready to work through all those births, nothing discouraged him. But the first man felt that even four more births were too long. Only perseverance, like that of the man who was willing to wait aeons brings about the highest result.